THE BRIDGE OF SECRETS

The Murder of Evelyn Hartley

Linda Davidson

*For Evelyn—and for every family still waiting
by a window in the dark.*

"Rivers remember what people forget."

— FROM A LA CROSSE SEARCHER'S FIELD NOTE, 1953

CONTENTS

ABOUT THE AUTHOR

Linda Davidson writes investigative true crime with an unwavering commitment to ethics, evidence, and the human cost that lingers long after the headlines fade. Her work centers victims as people—not plot points—and follows cases with a clear-eyed focus on what can be proven, what was claimed, and what was quietly misunderstood.

With a style that reads with the momentum of a thriller but the discipline of a record, Davidson examines how public narratives form: how rumor hardens into "truth," how media framing shapes empathy, and how perception can steer investigations, trials, and even memory itself. She traces the turning points—missed chances, breakthroughs, courtroom battles—while never losing sight of the families and communities forced to live inside the aftermath.

To explore all of Linda Davidson's books and new releases, visit her Amazon Author Page on Kindle: Linda Davidson.

LIST OF ILLUSTRATIONS

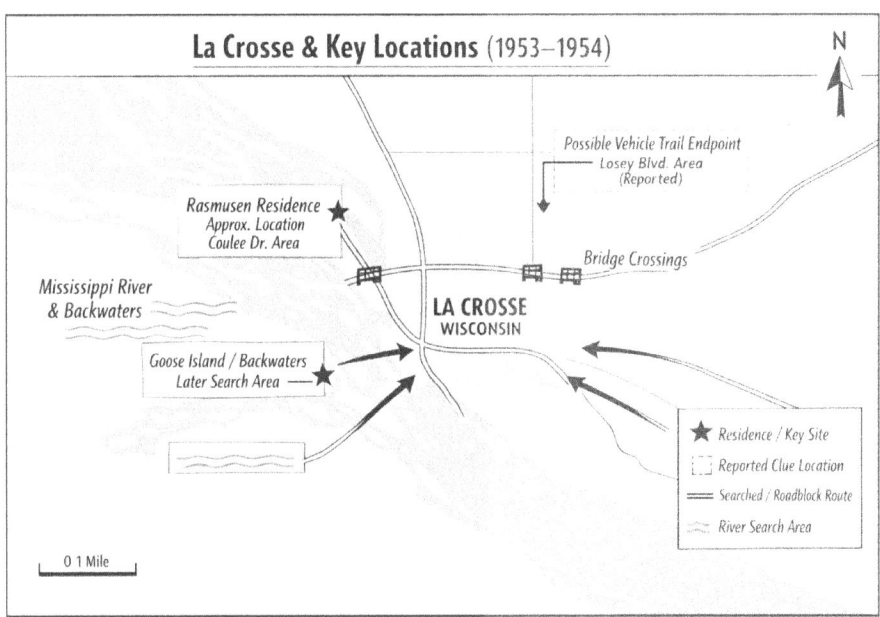

Map of La Crosse & Key Search Sites (1953–1954)

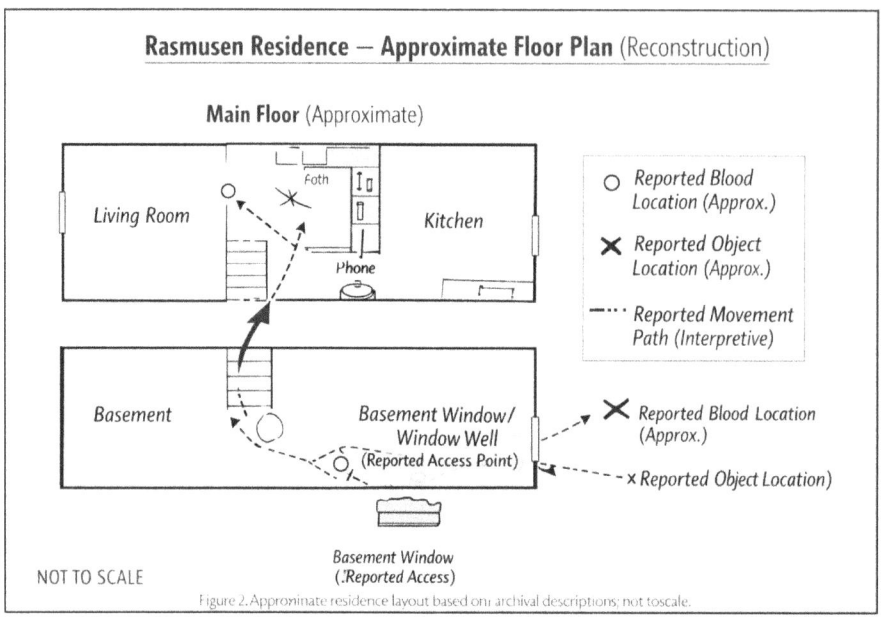

Rasmusen Residence—Approximate Floor Plan (Reconstruction)

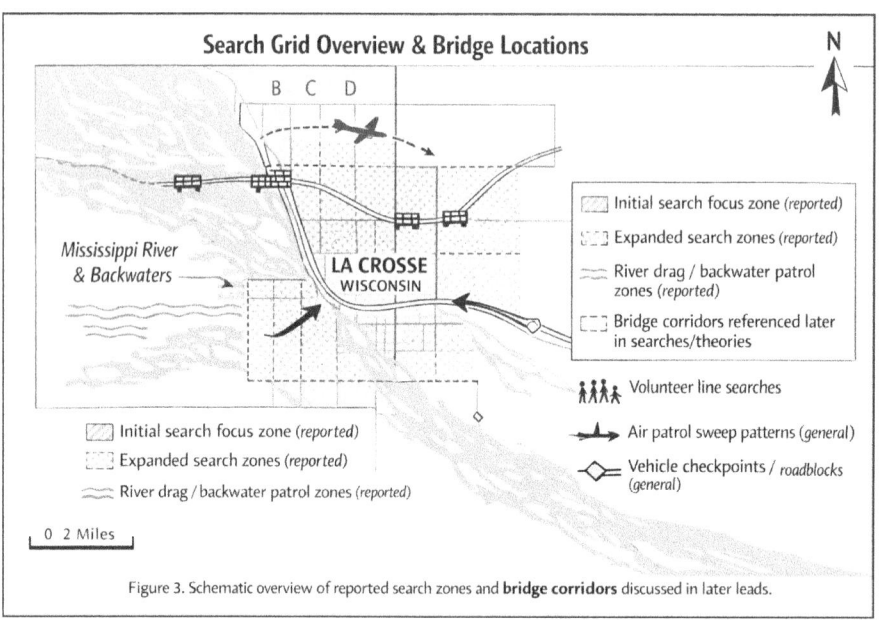

Search Zones and Bridge Locations

PREFACE

When I first opened the archival box labeled Cold Case 53-10 — HARTLEY, EVELYN GRACE, I expected what most people imagine when they hear the words cold case: yellowed pages, brittle photographs, typed reports softened by age. I expected a record.

What I didn't expect was the feeling of a town inside a box.

The first items were practical—forms, statements, sketches, evidence logs. But as I turned the pages, it became clear that this file contained more than documentation. It held the fingerprints of a community that refused to let a girl disappear quietly. In the margins of reports, you could sense urgency. In the repetition of search notes, you could feel exhaustion. In the careful preservation of fragments that seemed, at the time, too small to matter—blood stains, glass, a broken pair of glasses—you could see a belief that the future might be kinder to the truth than the past had been.

That belief is part of what brought me here.

This book is not only about what happened to Evelyn Hartley. It is also about what happened to La Crosse in the wake of her disappearance: the routines that changed, the trust that shifted, the way fear settled into ordinary life and refused to leave. It is about the long arc of an investigation that moved through eras—through the limitations of 1950s forensics, through the evolving language of law enforcement, through decades of rumors and revivals—while one simple fact remained unchanged: Evelyn never came home.

I wrote this with two commitments.

The first is commitment to **the record**. Where the archival sources speak clearly, I follow them closely. I favor contemporaneous reporting and verified public documentation. When details conflict, I acknowledge the conflict. When certainty is not possible, I do not manufacture it.

The second is commitment to **restraint**. True crime has the power to illuminate—but it can also exploit. This story is not told to sensationalize violence or to turn suffering into spectacle. Survivors are treated with care. Private individuals are not named where doing so would cause harm or mislead. And while this book uses narrative techniques to carry readers into the atmosphere of an era—the cold air of October, the hush of a neighborhood at night—those techniques are not a substitute for evidence. They exist to help us understand context, not to claim knowledge we do not have.

A cold case is often described as a mystery. But for the families who live inside it, mystery is not entertainment. It is a form of weight—carried quietly, year after year, in the absence of answers.

Evelyn Hartley was not a headline. She was a fifteen-year-old girl with a life unfolding in front of her. She was loved. She mattered. And the fact that her story remains unresolved is not a reason to look away—it is a reason to look more carefully, more honestly, and more humanely.

If remembrance has power, may this work help carry Evelyn's name a little farther.

Note to the Reader

This book addresses abduction, violence, and grief with care. If you need support, consider connecting with local victim-services organizations and national missing-persons resources listed in the back matter. Proceed at your own pace.

— **Linda Davidson**

DISCLAIMER

This book is a narrative work of nonfiction drawn from publicly available information, including archival newspaper reporting, historical summaries, and other secondary sources. Every effort has been made to verify names, dates, locations, and investigative details through cross-checking available records and relying on the most contemporaneous reporting where possible.

Because this case spans many decades, some details remain disputed, incomplete, or inaccessible. Records may conflict, memory-based accounts may vary, and certain original materials may be missing, sealed, or degraded by time. Where the historical record is unclear, the text reflects that uncertainty rather than presenting speculation as fact.

To protect privacy and minimize harm, this book avoids naming private individuals who were never charged or convicted, and it omits or generalizes identifying details where appropriate. Survivors and their families are treated with restraint and respect. Descriptions of violence are not included for shock value; the focus remains on impact, accountability, and the long-term consequences of trauma and fear.

This book is not intended to provide legal, medical, clinical, or therapeutic advice. Readers who find any content distressing are encouraged to prioritize their wellbeing and seek support from a qualified professional or local victim-services resources.

Despite careful research and editing, errors or omissions are possible. They are unintentional and will be corrected in subsequent editions upon receipt of verified information.

EVIDENCE & TIMELINE

- **Date/time:** Saturday, **Oct 24, 1953** (homecoming). Evelyn vanishes while babysitting at the Rasmusen home.
- **Scene indicators:** forced entry signs at a basement window well; footprints; moved furniture; blood traces; missing eyeglass lens.
- **Child unharmed:** the toddler slept through the event.
- **Post-crime finds:** items of clothing with blood located at different spots; blood type matched Evelyn's (serology era).
- **Response:** massive searches; vehicle inspections; grave re-opens; later, controversial polygraph sweep of students.
- **Later lead (1969 tape; public 2004):** alleged self-implication of Peterson & Gaulphair, claim of burial near La Farge; no confirmed recovery.
- **Ed Gein:** questioned/cleared; persistent myth persists due to pop culture.

PROLOGUE

— Friday Night Lights

La Crosse, Wisconsin.

Friday, October 24, 1953. The night air carried the crisp bite of autumn—the kind that made the homecoming crowd huddle closer under the stadium lights at Memorial Field. The band blared the school's fight song, and the stands pulsed with teenage energy. It was a night that should have been remembered for touchdowns, cheers, and the glow of small-town pride. Instead, it would be remembered for something else entirely—the night fifteen-year-old Evelyn Grace Hartley vanished without a trace.

Evelyn wasn't at the game. She had promised her parents she'd stay in for the night, but when another girl, also a babysitter, canceled at the last minute, Evelyn agreed to help. The Rasmusens were a well-known family—Viggo Rasmusen taught at La Crosse State College—and they needed someone responsible to watch their toddler while they attended the homecoming events. Evelyn, reliable and conscientious, seemed the perfect choice.

It was supposed to be a quiet night. A movie on the small television, a phone call to check in with her parents around eight, and maybe a bit of homework once the little boy was asleep. Nothing out of the ordinary. But as the evening stretched on, a silence began to form—first unnoticed, then unsettling.

Her father, Richard Hartley, was used to Evelyn calling when she babysat. She always checked in. By 10:30, he began to worry. The stadium lights were going out by then, the streets emptying. He called the Rasmusen home several times, but no one answered. Uneasy, he drove across town.

The Rasmusen house sat on the edge of a quiet neighborhood on Coulee Drive, the kind of place where porch lights marked safe familiarity. But when Mr. Hartley arrived, something felt off. The doors were locked, the shades drawn. He circled the house, calling Evelyn's name softly at first, then louder. No answer. He knocked, then peered through a window—and saw an overturned table and a pair of shoes that didn't belong where they were.

He found a way in through an unlocked back door. Inside, the stillness was suffocating. The toddler slept soundly upstairs, untouched by whatever had taken place below. But the living room told a different story. Furniture was moved, one window's screen lay on the floor, and a pair of Evelyn's eyeglasses sat broken nearby—one lens missing entirely. Then came the most chilling discovery: a small smear of blood on the walls, another on the floor near the basement steps.

Richard called the police.

By midnight, the Hartley home was filled with frantic whispers and flashlights. Officers from the La Crosse Police Department, joined later by the county sheriff's office, began documenting what would become one of Wisconsin's most confounding missing persons cases. They scoured the house, the yard, and the nearby fields, trying to piece together the unthinkable.

Outside, the neighborhood buzzed awake as word spread. Someone had taken a girl—right from the heart of La Crosse. It seemed impossible. This wasn't Chicago or Milwaukee. This was a quiet river town where doors were left unlocked and everyone knew each other by name.

Investigators quickly pieced together a tentative timeline. Evelyn had arrived at the Rasmusen house around 6:45 p.m. She was last seen by a neighbor around 7:15, moving through the living room. Her father's first unanswered call came at 8:30. By the time he arrived, somewhere between 10:45 and 11:00, Evelyn was gone.

No one had seen a car pull up. No one heard a struggle. Yet signs of violence were unmistakable. Blood led from the living room to the backyard, and there were impressions in the soft earth near a basement window well—as if someone had climbed in or out.

The police chief called it an abduction before dawn broke. By morning, hundreds of volunteers joined the search—police officers, Boy Scouts, soldiers from Fort McCoy, and residents who combed fields, ditches, and barns in the hope of finding any trace of Evelyn. The La Crosse Tribune printed her picture across the front page: a smiling girl with dark hair and bright, intelligent eyes. Beneath it, the words *"High School Girl Missing After Babysitting Job."*

For weeks, the town searched. Bloodhounds picked up faint trails that vanished near the highway. Planes circled overhead. Checkpoints stopped hundreds of cars, inspecting trunks and seat covers for blood. Every field, riverbank, and culvert within twenty miles was scoured. Yet nothing—no body, no clothing, no resolution—was ever found.

Evelyn Hartley had simply disappeared.

Theories began to swirl almost immediately. Some whispered that a drifter had passed through town. Others were convinced the crime was local—someone who knew her schedule, her route, her reliability. For years, police would chase tips that led nowhere, and names that faded with time. A shattered pair of glasses and a few bloodstains became all that remained of her last known moments.

Still, La Crosse could never let her go. Generations later, people would speak of her in hushed tones—*"the babysitter girl," "the one who vanished that night."* Her story lingered in the town's memory like an unfinished sentence.

And though decades have passed, the case has never been officially closed. Somewhere out there—perhaps in an unmarked grave near the Driftless hills, or beneath the silt of the Mississippi—lies the truth of what happened to Evelyn Grace Hartley.

The bridge between the known and the unknown still stands, weathered but unbroken. It connects the innocent promise of a homecoming night to the dark silence that followed—a bridge of secrets waiting to be crossed.

CHAPTER 1 A HOUSE OUT OF PLACE

The Sirens at Dawn

In the pale light of dawn on October 25, 1953, La Crosse awoke to the sound of police sirens echoing down Coulee Drive. What had begun as a worried father's search for his daughter had escalated into a full-scale criminal investigation. The Rasmusen home—an unassuming, two-story structure surrounded by manicured hedges and maple trees—was now sealed off with ropes and guarded by uniformed officers. Inside, detectives moved cautiously, their flashlights catching fragments of what was once a quiet evening in progress.

There was no forced door. No shattered lock. Yet every room spoke of interruption.

The Living Room: Signs of Sudden Violence

The living room bore the most obvious signs of struggle. A table lamp was overturned, its shade crushed underfoot. Magazines scattered across the floor. A sofa cushion lay discarded by the stairs. And near the north window—where the screen had been neatly removed—lay a pair of black-rimmed eyeglasses, one lens shattered, the frame slightly bent. They were Evelyn's.

The Kitchen and the First Blood

In the kitchen, officers found smudged fingerprints along the counter and a chair slightly out of place, as if someone had brushed against it hastily. But what chilled them most were the stains. On the carpet near the basement door, faint but unmistakable, was a trail of blood—small at first, then smeared, as though something or someone had been dragged or carried through.

Sergeant Francis Harpole, one of the first officers on scene, later described the sight as "quiet chaos." Nothing had been looted, yet nothing looked right. A half-eaten sandwich still sat on a plate by the sink, next to a glass of milk beginning to separate. The phone hung slightly off its cradle, as if dropped mid-dial. Every detail suggested a moment violently cut short.

The Basement Window

Downstairs, in the basement, the air felt colder. Officers noted scuff marks on the concrete floor near a small window well—the same one found open from the outside. Beneath it, bits of grass and dirt clung to the wall. Someone had entered or exited here. Nearby, another spot of blood marked the lower step, tiny but clear in the beam of a flashlight.

The Sleeping Child Upstairs

Upstairs, the toddler Evelyn had been watching slept peacefully in his crib, undisturbed through whatever terror had unfolded below. It was both a miracle and a riddle—how could a violent abduction have occurred without waking a child or alerting the neighbors?

The Yard and the Lost Footprints

Outside, police cordoned off the yard and began photographing every angle of the house. The yard sloped gently toward the alley, where a few footprints were discovered—one set small, possibly Evelyn's; another larger, pressed deeper into the soil. The impressions were photographed but, by the following day, trampled by the army of searchers who flooded the scene. The 1950s were not kind to evidence preservation.

The Dogs and the Vanishing Scent

Detectives called in bloodhounds from nearby Fort McCoy. The dogs picked up a trail that led through the yard, across the street, and toward a small wooded area—but it abruptly stopped near Losey Boulevard. Some said it ended where a car might have been parked. Others swore the dogs were confused by the growing crowd. Either way, the scent disappeared into nothing.

A Timeline of Uncertainty

By sunrise, the Rasmusen home had become the focal point of a mystery that defied logic. A babysitter had vanished from a locked house on a calm Friday night, in a neighborhood where every porch light was still burning. The only certainty was that something terrible had happened within those walls.

Inside police headquarters, a timeline began to take shape:

6:45 p.m. — Evelyn arrives at the Rasmusen home

7:15 p.m. — A neighbor sees her moving inside the living room

8:30 p.m. — Richard Hartley's first call goes unanswered

10:30 p.m. — Second unanswered call; he drives over

11:00 p.m. — Discovery of the disturbed house

Every minute between those times now belonged to speculation.

Early Witnesses and First Rumors

Officers canvassed the area, knocking on doors, asking if anyone had heard screams or seen a stranger. One woman recalled a car idling near the street around nine o'clock, but she couldn't describe the make or driver. Another claimed she noticed a man walking briskly away from the neighborhood, wearing dark clothing. None of it could be confirmed.

The Case Spreads Beyond La Crosse

Within hours, dozens of volunteers joined the effort. College students, teachers, factory workers—ordinary citizens combed the surrounding fields and riverbanks. Police radioed nearby towns, alerting them to watch for any vehicle carrying two or more people acting "suspiciously nervous." The case spread across county lines before the first newspaper even hit the stands.

Evidence Collection and Its Limits

Back at the house, evidence collection continued late into Saturday afternoon. Officers bagged the broken eyeglasses, a small piece of bloodied cloth found near the basement, and soil samples from outside the window well. In 1953, the best they could do was type the blood, not identify it. It would later match Evelyn's— Type O—but so did that of half the population.

The window screen, strangely, had been set carefully against the side of the house, not torn or bent. Whoever removed it knew what they were doing. There were no clear fingerprints, only partial smudges.

Theories Begin to Form

Neighbors whispered theories. Some said Evelyn had been targeted, that someone had followed her from school or seen her at the store earlier that day. Others suggested a random burglary gone wrong. But there were inconsistencies in both ideas. No valuables were missing, and the careful handling of the window suggested planning, not panic.

A House That Would Never Be Ordinary Again

By nightfall, searchers had covered nearly every inch of land within two miles of the home. They found nothing—no body, no discarded clothing, no sign of struggle beyond what was already known. It was as though Evelyn had been lifted out of her own life and erased.

The Rasmusen house was just another middle-class home in mid-century America, tidy and predictable. Yet something unspeakable had unfolded within its walls.

And from that day forward, for the people of La Crosse, it would never again be just a house.

It would be **the house where Evelyn disappeared**.

CHAPTER 2 THE ALARMS GO OFF

A Town Awakens to Fear

The morning of October 25, 1953, broke cold and gray over La Crosse. In a town used to the steady rhythm of Midwestern life—church bells, train whistles, factory shifts—the news spread like wildfire: A fifteen-year-old girl was missing. By sunrise, the case had already escaped the confines of the Rasmusen home and spilled into every street, every coffee shop, every living room.

At police headquarters, the telephones rang without pause. Officers from neighboring towns called to offer assistance. Volunteers began lining up before the morning briefing had even begun. Teachers from La Crosse State College, friends of Professor Rasmusen, joined the effort. So did the Hartleys' neighbors, students, and complete strangers who couldn't fathom a girl vanishing from a quiet home in their midst.

Mobilizing the Largest Search in County History

Chief Alforta ordered the largest search in county history. By noon, more than 1,000 people had assembled. The Civil Air

Patrol was summoned, along with National Guard units. Lines of volunteers fanned out across the coulees, cornfields, and wooded ridges surrounding the city. The search was methodical—shoulder to shoulder, eyes to the ground—but the tension in the air was palpable.

At first, they hoped Evelyn might still be alive—injured, disoriented, hiding somewhere. But as hours passed and nothing turned up, optimism turned to unease.

Roadblocks, Bloodhounds, and the Vanishing Trail

The police established a command post inside the La Crosse Fire Department's garage. There, officers marked up maps with grease pencils, tracking each search grid and assigning teams. Bloodhounds worked tirelessly, occasionally raising hope with a bark or a tug of recognition, only for the trail to vanish on the asphalt roads leading out of town. One dog reportedly led officers to the edge of Losey Boulevard before circling aimlessly—where many believed a car had been waiting.

Cars became the new focus. If Evelyn had been abducted, the killer would need a vehicle to escape quickly and unnoticed. Officers set up roadblocks on every highway entering or leaving La Crosse. Each driver was questioned, every trunk inspected. At one point, nearly 700 vehicles were searched. It was the kind of operation usually reserved for escaped convicts or fugitives—not a missing teenage babysitter.

Evidence, Media Pressure, and a Shift in Theory

The press descended quickly. By Sunday afternoon, reporters from Madison, Milwaukee, and even Chicago had arrived, jostling for quotes from exhausted officers. The La Crosse Tribune ran its second front-page headline in two days:

"Police Fear Foul Play in Babysitter Disappearance."

The accompanying article included a description of Evelyn: 5 feet 7 inches tall, 125 pounds, brown hair, brown eyes. She had been wearing a pink sweater, white blouse, red corduroy slacks, and white socks. The paper urged anyone with information to call police immediately.

Tips began flooding in—hundreds of them. A couple reported seeing a car parked on a side road around 9 p.m. Another claimed they'd heard a woman scream. A farmer in Onalaska thought he saw a young girl walking along a fence line after dark. Each call was logged, checked, and—almost always—dismissed.

But one clue stood out. On Sunday afternoon, a bloody handprint was found on the wall near the basement window of the Rasmusen home. It was small, likely Evelyn's. The print trailed toward the yard before ending abruptly. That same day, police also located blood stains on the grass and the lower steps of the basement stairway.

Investigators believed Evelyn had been attacked inside the house, possibly near the basement door, and then carried or dragged through the open window to a waiting vehicle. The lack of a violent struggle elsewhere suggested she may have been subdued quickly—struck, restrained, or rendered unconscious. It was a chillingly efficient crime.

When Hope Gave Way to Uncertainty

By Sunday night, the community had transformed into an extension of the investigation. Restaurants offered free coffee to searchers. Churches held vigils. The La Crosse Boy Scouts volunteered to comb through roadside ditches with flashlights. Men borrowed lanterns from gas stations and kept searching long after dark.

And still—nothing.

Detectives began visiting local schools on Monday morning. They questioned classmates, teachers, and anyone who might have known Evelyn's routines. The idea that a stranger had taken her seemed less likely the more they learned. Evelyn was responsible, cautious, and not the kind to open a door for anyone she didn't know.

The working theory shifted. Maybe the intruder wasn't a stranger at all.

Investigators looked closely at men who had recently done work in the neighborhood—handymen, delivery drivers, part-time repairmen. One by one, they were questioned and, if anything seemed amiss, sent for polygraph tests. Within days, more than 200 local men had been tested, including college students and even faculty members.

The searches extended beyond city limits. Airplanes from the Civil Air Patrol began flying low over the Mississippi River and its backwaters. Boats patrolled near the bridges. Searchers waded through reeds and sandbars.

Still nothing. No clothing. No weapon. No body.

Each passing day deepened the ache of uncertainty. The Hartleys clung to hope, though privately they began to understand the grim reality.

By the end of that first week, the case file was already inches thick —heavy with paper, heavier with silence.

Chief Alforta stood before the press once again and said:

"We have no suspect, no body, and no crime we can yet prove— only a missing girl and signs of violence."

As the sun set on the seventh day, volunteers lit lanterns along the bluffs, their lights flickering against the hills.

And the question remained—quiet, unbearable, unanswered:

Where was Evelyn Hartley?

CHAPTER 3 BLOOD ON THE STEPS

From Hope to Resignation

By the second week of Evelyn Hartley's disappearance, the tone inside La Crosse police headquarters had changed. The air of urgent optimism that had marked the first forty-eight hours was gone, replaced by exhaustion and something darker — resignation. Every officer in the building had walked through the Rasmusen home, studied the photographs, memorized the maps. They no longer talked about "if" something bad had happened to Evelyn. They talked about "where."

The shift began with blood — small, faint, and scattered, yet impossible to ignore.

The Crime Lab and the First Confirmation of Violence

On the morning of October 26, technicians from the Wisconsin State Crime Lab arrived to document and collect physical evidence. They began with the basement stairs. The wood was old, painted over several times, but near the lower steps, dark flecks stood out. Under light, the stains took on a dull brown hue

— blood. Drops trailed upward, smeared across the grain, as if someone had been carried past. Another small patch appeared at the base of the stairs near the furnace.

A laboratory test later confirmed what everyone already feared: the blood was human.

There was more on the living room rug — a thin line, barely visible unless the light struck it right — and another stain on the exterior wall near the open basement window. The screen leaned neatly against the house, its edges clean, its mesh intact. Whoever had removed it hadn't done so in panic.

Reading the Scene: A Crime Without Chaos

The pattern of evidence told a story — but an incomplete one.

If Evelyn had been attacked inside, why wasn't there more blood? Why was the furniture only slightly disturbed? Investigators theorized that the attack had been swift, precise, and that she had been subdued before she could scream. Perhaps she'd been struck from behind while walking toward the basement, where the family stored laundry. The small bloodstains supported that theory.

Detectives also noted a partial shoeprint in the damp soil beneath the window well. It was larger than Evelyn's known shoe size — closer to a man's size 10 or 11. Unfortunately, before plaster casts could be taken, rain washed much of it away. A mistake that haunted investigators for decades.

On the basement floor, they found something else — faint streaks of blood leading toward the window. They didn't form a pool or trail wide enough to suggest she had been dragged far, but it was enough to imply that her body, or at least her clothing, had made contact with that surface. The pattern was inconsistent — a few smears, then nothing — as though the attacker had lifted her and carried her the rest of the way.

Lieutenant Erwin Ross, one of the lead investigators, remarked later, "It wasn't the scene of a long fight. It was the scene of something that happened fast, by someone who knew how to move quickly."

The Eyeglasses: Proof of Overpowering

The broken eyeglasses became the centerpiece of the evidence. Found near the living room window, they were Evelyn's prescription pair — and she could barely see without them. That meant when they fell, she had likely been overpowered.

Investigators later located the missing lens several feet away, caught between a chair leg and the rug. Crime lab analysis confirmed it matched the frame. Small flecks of blood were found on the corner of the lens — further proof of violence.

And yet, for all the careful examination, police faced a cruel truth: there was no body, no weapon, no witnesses. Only a collection of details that refused to form a complete picture.

The blood tests — the most advanced forensic method available in 1953 — identified the stains as Type O, consistent with Evelyn's blood. But blood typing could not confirm identity; it could only exclude. At the time, investigators described the evidence as "probably hers." In modern terms, it was barely enough to prove a crime had occurred.

False Leads and Fresh Wounds

In an effort to find something tangible, detectives widened the search for physical items beyond the home. On October 27, a farmer several miles south of La Crosse reported finding a pair of bloodstained undergarments and a brassiere near a gravel road. The items were turned over to police, who confirmed they were similar in size and style to what Evelyn's mother described her daughter wearing that night.

The discovery sent shockwaves through the investigation — until closer inspection revealed inconsistencies. The garments could not be conclusively linked to Evelyn, and no one could recall her owning that exact pattern. Within days, the lead cooled.

For the Hartley family, the damage was irreversible. Each false alarm reopened the wound, forcing them to confront hope and loss again and again.

Back at the Rasmusen home, the basement stairs were removed entirely and transported to the crime lab. Technicians scraped the wood for deeper samples, searching for answers embedded in the grain. For Evelyn's parents, the house had become unbearable — a place where safety had been replaced by absence.

When a Disappearance Becomes a Murder

As forensic work continued, the atmosphere in La Crosse shifted. Some residents bristled at the growing police presence. Others feared the person responsible was still living among them. Parents forbade daughters from babysitting. Hardware stores sold out of locks and window latches. The sense of communal trust fractured.

Investigators worked through the nights, often sleeping on cots at the station. They reviewed photographs again and again — the overturned lamp, the displaced cushion, the blood on the steps — searching for meaning in repetition. The crime scene spoke clearly in one respect: control. Whoever had taken Evelyn had subdued her, removed her, and vanished in under three hours.

That required strength, planning, and familiarity.

The case was formally reclassified as a probable homicide — despite the absence of a body. Newspapers followed suit, shifting their language from "disappearance" to "murder." For Evelyn's parents, the words were unbearable. But they were also unavoidable.

Police issued a public statement:

*"Evidence strongly indicates that the missing girl has
met with foul play. Blood found at the scene and nearby
areas suggests injury, possibly fatal. We are continuing
the investigation as a criminal matter."*

Across Wisconsin, the headlines spread. Elsewhere, it was just another tragic story. In La Crosse, it was the end of certainty.

At the end of that long week, Chief Alforta stood alone in the basement of the Rasmusen home, staring at the bloodstains on the steps before they were removed for testing. A reporter later said he remained there in silence for several minutes.

When asked what he had been thinking, Alforta answered quietly:

"That's where her story ended — and someone else's began."

CHAPTER 4
WISCONSIN'S
BIGGEST SEARCH

The mobilization

By the end of October 1953, La Crosse no longer resembled the quiet college town it had been only a week earlier. Soldiers in olive drab uniforms stood at intersections. Airplanes buzzed low overhead. The Mississippi River, once a peaceful divider between Wisconsin and Minnesota, had become a search line in what authorities were calling "the largest manhunt in Wisconsin history."

It was a scale the state had never seen for a single missing person. The search for fifteen-year-old Evelyn Hartley had drawn together law enforcement, the military, and an entire population desperate for answers.

Chief Alforta and Sheriff Art Stellner coordinated the operation from a makeshift command center at the La Crosse fire station.

Every available resource was tapped. National Guard units rolled in from Camp McCoy. The Civil Air Patrol dispatched pilots and spotters to fly grid patterns over the coulees, river bottoms, and farmland for miles around.

Over 2,000 volunteers joined—students, farmers, clergy, Boy Scouts, and factory workers. Men from nearby towns arrived with hunting dogs and flashlights, ready to walk shoulder to shoulder through the cold fields. Women gathered at community halls to prepare sandwiches and hot coffee for the searchers. In those first days, the entire city of La Crosse became a living map of compassion and fear.

The effort was methodical. Search grids were drawn over large topographical maps; red markers identified sectors that had been covered. Each team was assigned an area—fields, ravines, drainage ditches, and stretches of the Mississippi's edge. The air patrol called in sightings of clothing or debris, and ground crews investigated immediately.

When a faint splash of color appeared against the gray riverbanks, hearts leapt—only to sink again. Time after time, the "possible clue" turned out to be a discarded rag, a dead animal, or a child's toy carried downstream.

By the fifth day, the search extended fifty miles beyond La Crosse. Newspapers began comparing it to military operations. Trucks moved in convoys, search dogs rotated in shifts, and volunteers were logged in and out like soldiers. The Red Cross set up tents to warm frostbitten fingers and hand out coffee. Even the students from La Crosse State College, Evelyn's future alma mater, suspended classes for a day to join the effort.

The river and the bluffs

The geography itself was both ally and enemy. The Mississippi and its maze of backwaters created hundreds of places to hide evidence—or a body. The Driftless hills surrounding the town offered countless caves, sinkholes, and crevices. Searchers walked narrow deer trails and scrambled over limestone ledges, often tethered to one another by rope to keep from slipping.

Boats dragged weighted nets along the river's edge, where the current ran slow. Others probed drainage ponds and culverts with long iron hooks. The cold, brown water yielded nothing. Each evening, as the searchers returned, mud-caked and weary, the absence of discovery weighed heavier than exhaustion.

Reporters followed the operation closely, their stories filling front pages across the Midwest. The *La Crosse Tribune* published daily maps of the areas searched, turning the investigation into a community obsession. In taverns, people unfolded the newspaper and traced their fingers along the red lines, suggesting where police should look next.

One editorial read:

"Until she is found, none of us in La Crosse will truly sleep."

The checkpoints

Highways leading out of the city were turned into checkpoints, each manned by pairs of deputies with flashlights and clipboards. They stopped every car, inspected trunks, questioned drivers. "Where are you headed? Where are you coming from? Did you see anything unusual Friday night?"

Gas stations and repair shops were ordered to report any suspicious vehicles—especially those with fresh upholstery stains or torn seat covers. Car washes were quietly monitored. Mechanics were asked to note any recent attempts to clean interiors.

It was a logistical feat for 1953, and for weeks it turned daily life upside down. Yet the public didn't complain. Everyone wanted the same thing—to bring Evelyn home.

The false alarms

With a search of this magnitude came inevitable false leads. On November 2, a call came from Vernon County: hunters had found what looked like bloodstained clothing near a stream. Officers rushed to the site, only to discover it was animal blood from a recent deer kill.

Days later, a farmer near Onalaska reported finding a shoe that "looked like it belonged to a girl." It was size 9½—too large to be Evelyn's. Each lead was a new spark of hope quickly extinguished by the cold light of reality.

Even the river refused to give up its secrets. Divers, limited by 1950s equipment and visibility, groped through the murky bottom with little success. "If she's in there," one diver told a reporter, "she's buried in the silt, and we'll never find her until spring."

The toll

The scale of the operation began to wear on everyone involved. Officers hadn't been home in days. Volunteers showed up with blisters on their hands. Richard Hartley—Evelyn's father—joined the search whenever he could, trudging through mud, flashlight in hand, long after most had gone home. "I can't stop," he told a journalist quietly. "If I stop, I'll think."

At night, the search teams gathered at the fairgrounds to rest. Dozens of people knelt together in prayer circles, asking for strength, asking for a miracle. Ministers walked among them offering quiet words of comfort. The sense of unity was powerful —but so was the fear.

Small-town innocence had been replaced by an unspoken awareness: whoever had done this might still be among them.

National attention

By early November, the case had captured national headlines. *Life* magazine requested photographs. Radio commentators called it "the mystery of the missing babysitter." FBI consultants reviewed reports at the state's request, though the case remained under local jurisdiction.

Offers of help poured in from across the country—psychics, self-styled detectives, and well-meaning strangers. Letters arrived at the police station daily, claiming visions or "dream clues" of where

Evelyn could be found. Some drew elaborate maps; others pointed to caves, wells, or barns. Detectives, though skeptical, logged them all.

None led anywhere.

As the days turned into weeks, winter crept closer. The leaves along the bluffs turned brown, the air sharp with the smell of frost. Search operations slowed. The National Guard pulled out, the planes grounded. The volunteers returned to their lives. But for the Hartleys, and for the investigators who refused to close the file, the search never truly ended.

Inside the police station, Chief Alforta stood over a large map peppered with red pins and stared at the river winding like a black ribbon through the city. "We've looked everywhere," he said quietly to one of his deputies. "Everywhere but the truth."

No one replied. The room was silent except for the hum of the fluorescent lights.

The map on the wall looked full, but the space between the pins—that's where Evelyn was.

CHAPTER 5 TEEN LIE DETECTORS

The birth of the plan

By mid-November 1953, the once relentless search for Evelyn Hartley had slowed, but the investigation had not. Patrol cars no longer lined the riverbanks, and the National Guard had gone home, but inside La Crosse police headquarters, the lights burned through the night. Detectives sat around cluttered desks, their coffee gone cold, staring at a wall of photographs that had begun to feel like a mirror of failure.

The evidence was thin, the leads had evaporated, and the case—barely a month old—was already growing cold. The newspapers had shifted from sympathy to frustration. One editorial captured the mood:

"How can a girl vanish from a house full of clues, and no one be held to account?"

That question hung over the investigation like smoke. The community wanted answers, and the police were under pressure to produce them. So, when the idea of *mass polygraph testing* surfaced, it didn't sound unreasonable—it sounded like hope.

The polygraph was still a new and glamorous technology in the 1950s. In popular culture, it was the "truth machine"—a scientific marvel capable of exposing lies with needles and ink. Law enforcement across America was infatuated with it. To a public desperate for certainty, the polygraph was almost magical.

Captain Donald Wenz of the Wisconsin State Patrol suggested that perhaps the kidnapper had been a local—someone Evelyn knew. After all, there had been no forced entry at the Rasmusen house, only an open basement window carefully removed. That pointed to planning, not impulse. If the offender were local, someone must have noticed something off: an injury, a sudden trip, a nervous change in behavior.

Chief Alforta agreed. Together, they developed a plan both ambitious and unprecedented: to polygraph every young man who fit the general profile of a potential suspect.

The parameters were broad. Male. Between sixteen and twenty-one. Resident of La Crosse or nearby towns. Students at Central High School, Logan High, or the State College would be prioritized. By the time the list was compiled, it contained nearly **1,750 names**.

The idea was to eliminate suspects systematically. Each boy would be interviewed briefly, asked a few basic questions, and tested for deceptive responses about the night of October 24.

The testing begins

The first sessions were conducted in late November at La Crosse Central High School. One by one, teenage boys filed into a small room where a state investigator sat behind a folding table, the polygraph machine beside him like something out of a science-fiction movie—chrome, wires, ink drums scratching lines onto white paper.

Each boy was asked the same questions:

- "Do you know Evelyn Hartley?"
- "Were you at or near the Rasmusen home the night she disappeared?"
- "Did you see or talk to her that night?"
- "Do you know who took her?"

The examiner's calm voice contrasted sharply with the boy's pounding heart, the hiss of the machine marking every breath.

Some boys found it exciting—a chance to be part of a high-profile case. Others were terrified. "I'd never even met her," one young man later recalled in an interview. "But everyone said if you twitched wrong, they'd think you did it."

Parents were uneasy. Rumors spread that police were targeting innocent kids, that the tests weren't reliable. A few refused to let their sons participate. But most cooperated, wanting to help clear their community of suspicion.

In total, **about 300 polygraphs** were completed before the program was quietly scaled back. Not a single test produced a confession or even a credible lead. The results were inconclusive, vague, and in many cases, contradictory. The "truth machine," once hailed as the path to justice, became just another dead end.

The backlash

When the *La Crosse Tribune* broke the story that hundreds of teenage boys had been wired to lie detectors, the public reaction was mixed. Some praised the effort—proof, they said, that police were doing everything possible. Others called it harassment, a mass invasion of privacy.

Editorial letters poured in. "Our sons are not suspects," one mother wrote. "They are students, not criminals." Another reader shot back: "If your son is innocent, he has nothing to fear."

Behind closed doors, even some officers began to question the logic. Detectives had spent weeks chasing down readings that meant little. Heart rates rose because the boys were nervous, not because they were guilty. In an era before strict polygraph protocols, the margin for error was enormous.

Still, Chief Alforta defended the operation. "If it clears the innocent," he told reporters, "then we're one step closer to finding the guilty."

But it hadn't cleared anyone. It had only exhausted resources and trust.

A growing sense of futility

By December, the first snow covered the hills around La Crosse. The search parties were gone, replaced by the sound of boots crunching on frozen ground as detectives rechecked old sites. The basement window at the Rasmusen home had been boarded up, but investigators returned often, standing in silence as if hoping the house would finally speak.

The case file, now inches thick, was beginning to feel like a grave of its own. Witness statements. Polygraph charts. Blood-type reports. Photographs. None of it moved the case forward.

The only thing still active was rumor.

In coffee shops and beauty parlors, speculation ran wild. Some claimed Evelyn had been kidnapped and taken across state lines. Others swore she had been buried in one of the limestone caves along the bluffs. A few even whispered about darker things —rituals, drifters, satanic cults—but those whispers said more about the fears of a community than the facts of the case.

One theory gained quiet traction among the investigators: that Evelyn had been attacked by someone she knew slightly—perhaps a college student or acquaintance from church—someone who knew she was babysitting that night. The careful removal of the window screen, the lack of loud struggle, and the efficient escape all hinted at a perpetrator familiar with both the area and the victim.

But without new evidence, it remained just that—a theory.

The year ends

As 1953 gave way to 1954, the case of Evelyn Hartley settled into an uneasy limbo. The Christmas decorations in La Crosse glowed brightly that winter, but for the Hartley family, the light meant little. Evelyn's presents sat unwrapped beneath the tree. Her mother could not bring herself to pack away her daughter's clothes. Her father stopped speaking to reporters altogether.

The city moved forward because it had to. Schools reopened, the Rasmusen family returned to their home, and the headlines faded beneath new stories. But beneath the surface, the unease remained.

The polygraph program had not found the truth. If anything, it had proved how elusive truth could be.

In later years, criminologists would cite the Hartley investigation as an early example of "polygraph overreach," a case where faith in technology outpaced understanding of its limits. But in 1953, those officers had only one goal—to find a missing girl—and they had used every tool available to them, even the ones that didn't work.

As winter settled hard over La Crosse, the case that had once commanded a state's attention became a whisper in the cold.

But the truth was still out there, somewhere in the dark hills, the frozen river, or the silence between neighbors who had stopped trusting each other. And in the files that now lined the police station walls, a note was scrawled across one officer's margin:

"When the ground thaws, we start again."

CHAPTER 6
EVIDENCE LOG

The Scene of the Crime

By the spring of 1954, the investigation into Evelyn Hartley's disappearance had entered a stage that police quietly referred to as "the waiting period." The snow had melted, the rivers had swollen with spring runoff, and searchers were once again combing through the ditches and woods along the Mississippi Valley. But as weeks turned into months, one thing became painfully clear: the case was running on evidence that told a story—but not a complete one.

The files from that winter, stacked high in the police archives, read like a ledger of uncertainty. Every item, every photograph, every stain, every footprint was catalogued meticulously—yet none of it had delivered the answer that everyone needed.

What follows is the evidence as investigators saw it then—and as forensic experts see it now.

The Rasmusen residence at 2431 Coulee Drive was a two-story, wood-frame home—ordinary by every standard of mid-century La Crosse life. But what police encountered there on the night of October 24, 1953, was anything but ordinary.

Inside, nothing was stolen. Jewelry, cash, and valuables remained untouched. There was no sign of vandalism. The house was locked except for the open basement window. The dining table had been moved slightly, and a lamp lay on its side. Evelyn's shoes were found by the sofa—aligned neatly, not kicked off in panic. That small detail, officers noted, was haunting. It implied she had either been attacked suddenly or had trusted whoever entered.

The only signs of violence were small and precise: a few scattered drops of blood, a broken pair of eyeglasses, a smudge near the basement steps, and faint streaks of blood on the floor leading toward the window well. The window screen, removed without tearing, leaned neatly against the exterior wall. Whoever had taken Evelyn had done so carefully, deliberately, and with confidence.

The Blood Evidence

At the time, blood analysis was limited to basic serology— determining blood type through antigen testing. The results confirmed the blood found inside the house and on the basement steps was **Type O**, the same as Evelyn's. However, the test could not prove the blood was hers. In 1953, Type O accounted for nearly half the population.

Samples were taken from:

- The living room rug (small smear)
- The basement stair riser (larger stain)

- The grass outside the window well (drops and partial streaks)

The stains were consistent with moderate bleeding, possibly from a head wound or nose injury, but not catastrophic trauma. That fact left open the possibility that Evelyn had been alive when taken from the house.

Today, those stains—if preserved—could be subjected to mitochondrial and nuclear DNA testing. Even degraded samples can yield genetic profiles. But in 1953, such technology was unthinkable. To investigators then, the blood was a clue without a voice.

The Broken Glasses

Perhaps the most personal piece of evidence was Evelyn's eyeglasses. She was nearsighted and rarely removed them except to sleep. They were found near the north window, the frame bent, one lens missing. The lens was later found under a chair, bearing a minuscule smear of blood. This confirmed that she had been attacked or at least jostled with force.

For detectives, the glasses told a devastating story. Evelyn had been caught off guard—perhaps while checking a noise, or while answering a knock. When the glasses fell, she would have been nearly blind. Whoever was in that room next had complete control.

The Basement Window and Prints

The basement window was small, set low to the ground. The screen was intact, not slashed, and removed with care. Soil beneath the sill showed a faint shoeprint—men's size 10 or 11, estimated. Unfortunately, rain and human activity destroyed the impression before casts could be taken. Another partial footprint was photographed on the basement floor, but the pattern was indistinct.

Investigators noted that the window could be opened from the outside only with difficulty. It was possible, but required familiarity with the latch mechanism—a detail that hinted the intruder might have known the house layout. Professor Rasmusen confirmed that only family members and a few maintenance workers knew about that particular latch.

If the crime occurred today, forensic technicians would likely recover touch DNA or latent prints from the window frame and screen. Even skin cells left behind could reveal a full profile. But in 1953, the tools didn't exist. The window was dusted with black powder, revealing only partial smudges—none usable for identification.

The Trail of Blood Outside

Police dogs had traced Evelyn's scent across the backyard, through a patch of grass, and toward Losey Boulevard—where it abruptly ended. Officers believed a vehicle had been parked there. The trail's sudden disappearance suggested she had been carried or placed into a car. Tire marks were found but were too faint to match to any specific tread pattern.

Modern investigators would photograph, cast, and measure every inch of those impressions. They'd extract soil samples, analyze microscopic fibers, and even search for automotive residue. In 1953, they took a few photographs and moved on.

That single oversight—failing to preserve the ground—likely erased the best chance of identifying the kidnapper's vehicle.

The Clothing and False Finds

In the weeks following her disappearance, several pieces of women's clothing were discovered along rural roads and creeks around La Crosse and Vernon counties. Each find triggered renewed hope—and renewed heartbreak.

Among the items collected:

- A bloodstained brassiere found near a gravel road
- A pair of panties with human blood (Type O)
- Fragments of red corduroy fabric matching the color of Evelyn's slacks

None were definitively linked to her. Some were determined to belong to other cases or had been discarded months earlier. In hindsight, investigators recognized a painful truth: in the desperation to find Evelyn, every scrap of cloth became a possible clue, whether or not it had any connection.

The Fingerprints

Partial fingerprints were recovered from the kitchen counter and the living room door frame. Most were smudged or overlapped with household prints belonging to the Rasmusens. The few usable ones were run through state files but matched no one. At the time, there was no national fingerprint database—only paper cards and manual comparisons. The FBI was consulted but found no match in their files either.

Those latent prints, if preserved, could today be digitized, enhanced, and run through national systems like AFIS or CODIS. But after decades of storage, it's uncertain whether any of the original lifts still exist.

The Witness Accounts

The eyewitness accounts were as frustrating as the physical

evidence.

- A neighbor saw Evelyn moving inside around 7:15 p.m.
- Several residents reported hearing dogs barking between 8:00 and 9:00 p.m.
- One motorist described a car parked with its lights off near Coulee Drive around 9:30.
- Another claimed to have seen a man walking briskly near Losey Boulevard.

Each sighting was plausible—but none were corroborated. In the absence of modern surveillance or doorbell cameras, there was no way to verify any of it.

The False Confessions and Dead Ends

Over the following months, police received more than a dozen false confessions. Some were attention-seekers; others were mentally ill. Each was investigated, and each fell apart under questioning. Years later, even notorious murderer Ed Gein would be questioned, though no evidence connected him to the case.

Every false confession drained manpower and morale. Each time a man claimed to know where Evelyn was buried, officers would rush to dig, search, and come up empty. The city began to feel cursed by its own hope.

What We Know vs. What We Don't

What We Know:

- Evelyn Hartley was attacked while babysitting at the Rasmusen home.
- Blood matching her type was found inside and outside the house.
- There were clear signs of abduction through the

basement window.

- A vehicle was likely used.
- The abduction occurred between approximately 7:15 and 10:45 p.m.

What We Don't Know:

- Who entered the home.
- How they gained knowledge of Evelyn's location that night.
- Whether more than one person was involved.
- What happened after she left the house.
- Where her remains are today.

The Modern Perspective

If the Hartley case were investigated today, it would look radically different. DNA testing could analyze trace evidence on the window screen, basement floor, or clothing. Luminol could map the path of blood invisible to the naked eye. Surveillance cameras and cell tower pings would trace movements. A digital database could instantly compare fingerprints, shoe impressions, and vehicle data across states.

In 1953, investigators worked with magnifying lenses, typewriters, and instinct.

Yet even now, modern forensic experts reviewing the evidence agree: this was not a random attack. It bore planning, precision, and restraint. The offender knew the window could be accessed quietly, knew how to subdue a victim quickly, and left the house with no visible struggle. That suggested either familiarity or calculated opportunity.

If Evelyn's remains were ever recovered, they might still tell her story. Bone fragments could yield mitochondrial DNA. Soil beneath her nails could hold microscopic traces of where she was taken. Even a single hair could rewrite the record of what happened that night.

But for now, the evidence remains frozen in time—a jigsaw puzzle missing its center.

A Case Suspended Between Eras

The Hartley investigation exists in two worlds: one of the past, where science ended at blood typing and shoeprints, and one of the present, where technology might finally speak for the silent.

In La Crosse, that duality lingers. Each year, a few residents still place flowers near Coulee Drive, where the Rasmusen house once stood. They come not because they expect answers, but because the questions refuse to fade.

In the end, the evidence did not fail the investigators. The era did.

And somewhere, in the quiet gap between what is known and what is lost, lies the truth of what happened to Evelyn Hartley.

CHAPTER 7 THE ED GEIN DETOUR

Four years after Evelyn Hartley vanished from the quiet streets of La Crosse, another Wisconsin town woke to a horror that seemed almost biblical in its depravity. On November 16, 1957, in Plainfield—a farming community barely two hours east—police entered the home of a reclusive handyman named **Edward Theodore Gein**. What they found inside would scar the state's psyche forever.

The details were almost unspeakable: human remains fashioned into household objects, skulls used as bowls, and a severed head hanging in a burlap sack. Gein confessed to robbing graves and murdering two women, Bernice Worden and Mary Hogan. The press would soon christen him "The Butcher of Plainfield."

But for investigators in La Crosse, that name struck a different, more chilling chord—because for years, Evelyn Hartley's disappearance had haunted them. And as Gein's crimes unfolded, the question arose almost immediately: *Could he have been the one who took Evelyn?*

A Connection of Geography, Not Evidence

The rumor began within hours of Gein's arrest. The towns of La Crosse and Plainfield were both small, rural, and separated by only about 160 miles—a three-hour drive even on 1950s highways. Reporters from *The Milwaukee Journal* and *Chicago Tribune* speculated that Gein might be connected to other disappearances across Wisconsin. Evelyn's name appeared on nearly every list.

The logic seemed obvious. Gein preyed on women. Evelyn was young, female, and had vanished without a trace. Both crimes involved the meticulous handling of a victim's body—suggesting a calculated, even ritualistic, element. To a public reeling from the macabre details pouring out of Plainfield, linking Gein to Evelyn felt almost inevitable.

Within days, La Crosse police were deluged with calls. Neighbors whispered, "They've found him. The man who took the babysitter."

But inside the department, investigators weren't so sure.

Chief Alforta, still haunted by the open file, immediately contacted state officials. Two detectives were sent to Plainfield to interview Gein and examine his property firsthand. Their mission: to determine whether any physical evidence—clothing, jewelry, or personal effects—could be tied to Evelyn Hartley.

The Search of the Gein Farm

The Gein farm was an isolated, two-story farmhouse set deep in the marshy farmland of central Wisconsin. Police spent days cataloguing the grotesque artifacts within. They found partial remains of at least fifteen women, though most were confirmed to have come from local graves. Gein's victims, it appeared, were chosen for their resemblance to his deceased mother and exhumed in an effort to "rebuild" her image through the dead.

When investigators from La Crosse arrived, they carried photographs of Evelyn, lists of her clothing and belongings, and plaster models of her dental structure. They compared every skull and bone fragment on the property. None matched Evelyn's age or dental profile. No fabric matched the red corduroy pants or pink sweater she had worn that night.

They questioned Gein directly. He was cooperative in his eerie, detached way, answering questions softly, even politely. When asked if he knew anything about "a girl from La Crosse who disappeared while babysitting," he shook his head and said simply, "No. I never been to La Crosse."

To confirm, officers checked his known movements and employment records. Gein rarely left Plainfield. Neighbors described him as a man who avoided travel entirely. The only time he had ventured far from home, they said, was to buy hardware supplies or attend local farm auctions.

Gein even passed two polygraph tests concerning the Hartley case—remarkable, considering his guilt in two other murders. Investigators concluded that, while he was undeniably a killer, he was not *that* killer.

How Rumor Outran Fact

The problem was that public fear travels faster than forensic reports. Within days of Gein's arrest, national headlines declared:

"WISCONSIN FARMER MAY HOLD CLUES TO MISSING GIRL CASES."

The wording was vague, but the implication was powerful. Reporters needed a story that stretched beyond Plainfield, and the

Hartley case—unsolved, local, and tragic—fit the bill.

By the time La Crosse authorities publicly cleared Gein, the connection had already hardened in the public imagination. To this day, many who remember Evelyn's story still mention Ed Gein in the same breath.

It didn't help that Hollywood borrowed liberally from both crimes. *Psycho* (1960), *The Texas Chain Saw Massacre* (1974), and *Silence of the Lambs* (1991) all drew partial inspiration from Gein's pathology. Each new adaptation reinforced his myth as a bogeyman capable of any atrocity. And as those films spread, so too did the false connection to Evelyn Hartley.

For the people of La Crosse, the rumor became both comfort and curse. Comfort, because it offered an answer—however monstrous. Curse, because it closed the door on other possibilities.

What the Files Actually Say

Official documents from the Wisconsin Department of Justice, reviewed decades later, list Gein among dozens of persons of interest investigated in connection with Evelyn's disappearance. His entry is brief, almost dismissive:

"Edward T. Gein – Plainfield, WI. Investigated November 1957. Cleared of involvement. No physical evidence linking subject to case. Alibi confirmed by local witnesses."

No DNA, no blood, no possessions. Nothing of Evelyn's was ever found on his property. For all the gruesome trophies recovered from that house of horrors, not one belonged to her.

The only thread connecting Gein to Evelyn was geography—and fear.

A State Haunted by Two Crimes

The coincidence of timing ensured the link would never completely fade. Wisconsin, in those years, was a state still learning to reconcile its innocence with its violence. Two girls —one vanished into air, the other into a nightmare—became symbols of opposite ends of horror: the unknown and the unspeakable.

For investigators, however, the difference mattered. Gein had been caught. Evelyn's abductor had not. And so the Hartley case remained what it had always been—a wound without a face.

Detectives returned to their evidence files with renewed urgency. If Gein wasn't responsible, then who was? The relief of ruling out one monster only underscored the presence of another, still hiding in the shadows.

By the early 1960s, a new set of suspects would emerge— men whose names never made headlines, but whose whispered confessions would keep the case alive for decades.

But before those leads surfaced, the Gein detour left one lasting lesson: sometimes, evil has more than one face, and not all of them are caught.

CHAPTER 8 THE BAR-TAPE CONFESSION

For sixteen years after Evelyn Hartley vanished, La Crosse lived in a strange, uneasy rhythm—half acceptance, half refusal. The case was technically open but practically dormant. Detectives had retired, evidence had been boxed and shelved, and the Rasmusen home had long since changed owners.

Then, in 1969, a crackle of sound from a tavern tape recorder pulled the case back into the light.

The Night at the Tap Room

On a muggy July night in the small town of Soldiers Grove, Wisconsin, a local man named **Clyde "Tywee" Peterson** sat at the bar of the Driftless Tap Room, drinking heavily. He was forty-six, wiry, with a mechanic's hands and a temper that grew loud after midnight.

A few stools away, another regular—Harold Meyer—was testing a new portable cassette recorder, a novelty at the time. He'd brought it to the bar to capture a polka band playing earlier that evening. By the time the crowd thinned, Meyer had left the recorder running.

What it captured instead was something far darker.

On the hiss-filled tape, over the clink of glasses and the thud of pool balls, Peterson's voice cuts through:

"I done that babysitter in La Crosse. Hartley. That girl never screamed once."

A pause. Laughter. Someone says he's full of it. Peterson insists.

"We took her out by the river. She's there. Nobody ever looked in the right place."

The men at the bar laugh again, thinking it drunk talk. But Meyer kept the tape. Days later, uneasy about what he'd heard, he played it for a friend—who happened to know a deputy in Crawford County. Within a week, the recording was in the hands of the La Crosse Police Department.

The Investigation Reopens

When detectives first played the tape, the room went silent. They had lived with this case for years; many still carried Evelyn's photo in their wallets. The voice on the cassette was rough, slurred, but clear enough to make the hair rise on the back of their necks.

Clyde Peterson had a record—burglary, assault, petty theft. He had lived in and out of La Crosse County during the early 1950s. His name appeared once, faintly, in an old interview log: he'd been questioned briefly in 1953 after a neighbor claimed he owned a car resembling one seen near Coulee Drive. The lead went nowhere.

Now, sixteen years later, he was confessing in a bar.

Detectives located Peterson at a boarding house on the north side of La Crosse. He didn't resist arrest. At headquarters, he denied the confession, claiming he was "just talking tough." He said he'd never met Evelyn Hartley, never been near the Rasmusen home, and barely remembered the night in question.

When confronted with the tape, he laughed.

"You can't prove what a man says when he's drunk means nothing," he told them.

Analyzing the Tape

Forensics in 1969 were primitive by modern standards, but the police took the recording seriously. The State Crime Lab cleaned and amplified the sound, confirming the voice as consistent with Peterson's.

Transcripts of the key segment read as follows:

Peterson: "Me and a buddy, we watched her through that window. She was reading, sitting on the couch. When the folks came home, she was gone. Ha! They never found her, did they?"

Unidentified Male: "You're full of it, Tywee."

Peterson: "Ask down by Goose Island. She's there. Buried near the bridge."

That final line would haunt investigators for decades—*Buried near the bridge.*

Detectives spent days searching the area Peterson mentioned. Goose Island lay along the Mississippi's backwaters, thick with cattails and shifting mud. They dug near every bridge piling and drainage culvert they could access. Nothing.

Meanwhile, Peterson's statements shifted with every interview. One day he claimed involvement, the next he denied it. Sometimes he named an accomplice—"a guy named Joe, worked construction"—but could never provide a last name. He failed a polygraph test but passed another weeks later.

After months of questioning, the district attorney concluded there was insufficient evidence to charge him. The tape, while chilling, was legally worthless without corroboration. Peterson was released.

Why the Confession Lingered

Over time, the "bar-tape confession" became a legend in La Crosse law enforcement circles. Some officers dismissed it outright; others were convinced it was genuine.

Supporters of the confession theory pointed out:

- Peterson's vague description of the Rasmusen living room matched reality.
- He mentioned the basement window before newspapers reprinted those details.
- He seemed to know the name *Hartley*, not always included in brief local discussions by 1969.

Skeptics countered that bar gossip could easily supply those same facts. The case had been publicized for years; anyone could have known the details. And Peterson's claim about the burial site —"near the bridge"—was so broad it bordered on meaningless. There were dozens of bridges along that stretch of the Mississippi.

Still, investigators couldn't let it go. They re-interviewed Evelyn's surviving family, re-examined the evidence, and even reopened some storage boxes from 1953. The file grew thicker again, filled with transcripts, photographs, and maps dotted with red circles where digs had come up empty.

The Man Behind the Boast

To understand the confession, detectives had to understand the man.

Clyde Peterson was a drifter by temperament—a small-time criminal who bounced between odd jobs and jail cells. Those who knew him described a man desperate for attention, especially when drunk. "He liked to scare people," one former coworker said. "He'd brag about things just to see if you'd believe him."

Psychologists later labeled this pattern *false confessor syndrome*— the compulsion to claim involvement in notorious crimes for ego, notoriety, or delusion. It's the same phenomenon that produced over fifty false confessions in the Lindbergh kidnapping and dozens more in the Black Dahlia case.

Yet the possibility remained that Peterson's drunken words contained fragments of truth. Investigators noted that his timeline placed him living in La Crosse County in late 1953, doing carpentry work not far from Coulee Drive. His vehicle, a 1949 Chevrolet sedan, roughly matched a "dark car" seen near the Rasmusen home that night. But no physical link could be drawn.

When Peterson died in 1974, still denying involvement, detectives were left with nothing but that tape—and the hollow echo of his voice bragging into the dark.

Legacy of a Tape

The "bar-tape confession" became one of the most controversial artifacts in the Hartley case file. To some, it was the closest thing to closure La Crosse ever got. To others, it was just another cruel trick of coincidence—a man's drunken fantasy mistaken for confession.

Years later, digital audio engineers cleaned the original tape with modern software. The words were the same, but the tone was different. In the clarity of digital playback, Peterson didn't sound boastful. He sounded scared—his voice low, wavering, as though remembering something he wished he hadn't said.

Whether that fear came from guilt or alcohol, no one can say.

But even now, in the archives of the La Crosse County Sheriff's Department, the cassette remains sealed in an evidence envelope marked simply:

"Hartley Case — Tape #47 — Goose Island Confession."

A voice in a bar, a boast on tape, a bridge that hides its secrets.

CHAPTER 9 THE BRIDGE SEARCH

By the 1970s, the story of Evelyn Hartley had slipped from the headlines but never from the town's memory. Every so often, something would stir the waters again—a letter, a rumor, a confession, a discovery that seemed almost too coincidental to ignore. And nearly every time, it led back to the same place: the bridges.

The bridges of La Crosse had always been the city's most symbolic structures—spanning the Mississippi, connecting Wisconsin to Minnesota, holding thousands of quiet secrets beneath their girders. To those who searched for Evelyn, they were more than crossings. They were possibilities.

The theory that Evelyn's body had been hidden "near the bridge" began with the **bar-tape confession** of Clyde "Tywee" Peterson in 1969. It was a vague phrase, muttered between drinks, but investigators couldn't shake it. When he said "the bridge," locals assumed he meant the **Pettibone Bridge**, the most prominent crossing in the area—a long, steel-trussed structure shadowing the river between La Crosse and Pettibone Island. The other likely location, **Goose Island**, lay a few miles south, its marshland tangled with reeds and flood debris.

The two sites became the focal points of a search that would stretch across decades.

The 1970 Search: Beneath Pettibone

The first official search began in the summer of 1970, led by the La Crosse County Sheriff's Department with help from volunteer divers. The Mississippi was low that year, its backwaters slow and muddy—conditions that encouraged belief as much as they hampered progress.

Divers moved along the east bank near Pettibone Park, guided by a hand-drawn map someone claimed had been based on Peterson's drunken description. The water was opaque. Visibility was less than a foot. They worked by touch, feeling along submerged pilings and sandbars.

For days, they found nothing but the river's ordinary ghosts: rusted cans, bicycle frames, old tires.

Then, on the fifth day, a diver surfaced clutching what looked like a fragment of fabric—dark, fibrous, and stiff with age. Word spread instantly. Reporters gathered at the riverbank; the *La Crosse Tribune* ran the headline:

"Possible Break in Hartley Case — Divers Recover Cloth Near Pettibone Bridge."

The lab later determined the material was from a piece of canvas tarp, likely from a discarded boat cover. The excitement died as quickly as it had flared.

Still, that brief surge of hope revealed something deeper: La Crosse wasn't ready to let go. The community's collective memory had fossilized around Evelyn's name. Every new search became not only about finding her, but about absolving the town of the guilt that came from not having done enough.

Goose Island: A Landscape That Moves

In 1974, sheriff's deputies organized another search, this time near **Goose Island**, the area Peterson had specifically mentioned on the tape. It was a difficult place—part river delta, part forest, a shifting labyrinth of mud, cattails, and shallow channels. The island's shape itself changed each year with flooding, erasing any clear coordinates that could have mattered.

Searchers used long metal probes to test the soil for disturbed ground. Some spots gave way easily, others resisted like packed clay. More than once, a probe struck something solid—only to reveal driftwood or stone beneath the surface.

One volunteer, a retired firefighter named Walter Harris, later described the eerie quiet of that search:

"You'd be out there alone, up to your knees in muck, and the river would go still. Just still. And you'd start thinking—she's here. Somewhere right under your boots."

When the day ended, they'd wash off their boots, haul their equipment back to the trucks, and drive home in silence.

The Bridge Rumor Expands

As the years passed, the phrase "near the bridge" took on a life of its own. Some said Peterson meant Goose Island Bridge. Others believed he referred to **the old wagon bridge** that once connected La Crosse to French Island. Still others pointed to the smaller **railroad bridge** downstream, unused and overgrown.

Each new interpretation spawned a new round of searching. Theories layered upon theories, until "the bridge" became more symbol than location—an emblem of where truth and river both disappeared beneath the surface.

Throughout the 1980s, amateur investigators, retired officers, and true-crime enthusiasts returned to these banks with metal detectors and shovels. One private group used ground-penetrating radar near the southern levees in 1984, long before the technology was common in police work. They detected anomalies—pockets of disturbed soil—but when the county denied excavation permits due to environmental protections, the effort stalled.

It was as if the river itself was conspiring to keep its secret.

Fragments and False Hope

Occasionally, bone fragments surfaced along the river after storms—each time prompting a flurry of speculation. The county coroner examined dozens over the years. Most were animal. A few were too degraded to tell. None could be confirmed as human, and certainly not as Evelyn's.

One particularly emotional episode occurred in 1986, when a fisherman found a partial skull downstream near Brownsville, Minnesota, roughly twenty miles from La Crosse. The bone's size suggested a female teenager. For a week, the Hartley case returned to national headlines. Television crews descended on La Crosse, interviewing residents who still remembered that October night in 1953.

The hope ended when forensic testing identified the remains as belonging to a Native American woman from centuries earlier—an archaeological, not criminal, discovery.

Still, the moment mattered. It proved that, even after thirty years, the story could still stop time in La Crosse.

The Investigators Who Refused to Quit

Two men, in particular, refused to let the river silence Evelyn's story. Detective **John Burgess**, who joined the department in the late 1970s, and Sheriff **Vernon Clausen**, who had been a rookie in 1953, made a pact: as long as either lived, the case would never officially close.

They spent countless weekends revisiting files, cross-referencing maps, and driving to the river's edge with new theories. In the 1980s, they even consulted hydrologists at the University of Wisconsin to model how flood patterns might have shifted sediment around the bridges over the decades. The experts agreed that a burial in 1953 could easily be twenty feet deeper by then—possibly unreachable without major excavation.

"Somewhere under all that mud," Burgess said, "there's an answer. The question is whether we're still listening."

He was right. Over time, the town's listening grew quieter. The younger generation barely knew the name Evelyn Hartley, and the older ones had learned to whisper it only on anniversaries.

The Symbol of the Bridge

By the late 1980s, the search had become more symbolic than forensic. The bridge was no longer just a structure of steel and stone—it was a metaphor for the case itself. Something meant to connect had instead come to divide: between what was known and what could never be proved.

Each dive, each dig, each failed lead added another layer to the legend of "The Bridge of Secrets."

Standing on the Pettibone Bridge at dusk, you can still see how the Mississippi swallows its reflections whole. The water moves slow and heavy, concealing everything beneath its mirrored calm. Locals say if you listen closely on autumn nights, when the wind dies and the current hushes, you can hear the soft lapping that sounds like footsteps—like someone crossing, but never reaching the other side.

What Remained

By the end of the 1980s, official searches had stopped entirely. The Goose Island site was reclaimed by marshland. Pettibone Bridge underwent renovation, its girders sandblasted clean of decades of rust and graffiti.

The case file now weighed nearly forty pounds—a collection of every rumor, report, and hope ever recorded. Yet Evelyn herself remained a ghost in paper form: no body, no suspect, no resolution.

Still, those who worked the searches say they felt her presence. "It's like she's tied to this river," one diver recalled. "Every time I went down, I thought—she's watching, waiting for someone to see her."

The river, of course, never gave her back.

But it never forgot her either.

CHAPTER 10 A TOWN THAT NEVER FORGOT

In most towns, tragedies fade with time. Names slip from memory, stories lose their edges, and grief turns into folklore. But in La Crosse, Wisconsin, one name never faded.

Evelyn Hartley became more than a missing girl — she became a measure of innocence lost.

For decades after that October night in 1953, her disappearance continued to shape the rhythms, fears, and rituals of the city that failed to bring her home. Every parent who checked a lock twice, every girl who hesitated to take a babysitting job, every officer who joined the force in search of purpose — all carried a trace of her story.

Even without her body, Evelyn's absence became a presence that hovered over La Crosse like a memory that refused to end.

The Caution That Changed Childhood

Before Evelyn vanished, La Crosse was the sort of town where people left doors unlocked and waved to neighbors from front porches. Children roamed freely — to the ice cream shop, the park, the river. The city was built on trust, small enough that everyone believed danger lived *somewhere else.*

After October 1953, that belief evaporated.

Parents began driving their daughters to and from babysitting jobs. Families started leaving porch lights on all night. Schools held safety assemblies that warned students never to open doors to strangers, never to walk home alone after dark.

"It was like the air changed," one resident later recalled. "Before Evelyn, we thought we were safe. After Evelyn, we just hoped we were."

Newspapers coined a phrase that would echo through generations — *the babysitter murders.* It became a genre, a cultural shorthand for vulnerability in the suburbs. Years later, when horror films like *When a Stranger Calls* and *Halloween* hit theaters, La Crosse residents whispered that they knew where those stories began.

The line between caution and fear blurred, and in that blur, Evelyn's ghost lived on.

The Police Who Couldn't Let Go

For the La Crosse Police Department, the Hartley case became both burden and compass. Every new missing person report, every suspicious disappearance that crossed an officer's desk, carried an unspoken comparison: *Is this another Evelyn?*

Detectives who had been young men in 1953 carried the file like a moral anchor through their careers. Some kept copies of her photograph in their wallets, her dark hair and round glasses a reminder of why they joined the force.

Retired Detective **Vernon Clausen** would visit the evidence room on anniversaries, opening the file just to touch the papers, as if the act itself kept her alive. "I never saw it as an old case," he said in an interview years later. "I saw it as a promise we hadn't kept."

The unsolved case reshaped how police handled disappearances. No longer would a missing teenager be dismissed as a runaway. Within hours, full investigations began. Procedures changed, protocols hardened. The search for Evelyn, though unsuccessful, became a template for the future.

It taught a generation of officers the value of urgency — and the cost of waiting too long.

The Town That Carried Her Name

In La Crosse, landmarks and local stories began to quietly absorb her memory. Some residents refused to drive down **Coulee Drive** after dark. Others avoided the **Rasmusen house**, which later families swore held a heaviness that couldn't be explained.

Each Halloween, parents told their children the story — not as a ghost tale, but as a warning: *Be home before dark. Don't talk to strangers. Remember the babysitter who didn't come back.*

Civic groups organized safety programs in her name. One high school debate team once raised funds for a missing children's awareness campaign, calling it "The Evelyn Project." No official memorial stood for her, yet she was everywhere — in the way people locked their doors, in the way silence fell over a conversation when someone mentioned 1953.

Even the river seemed to carry her presence. On calm nights, when the water mirrored the city lights, locals swore they saw shapes that looked like footprints on the sandbars — as though someone had walked halfway across and vanished.

The Ripple of Fear and Faith

Evelyn's disappearance also left a deeper mark — one that lived inside people rather than policy. For some, it shattered faith in human nature; for others, it deepened it. Churches filled in the weeks after she vanished. Ministers preached about evil and innocence, about the fragility of life and the mystery of suffering.

"Some tragedies," one pastor said, "are not meant to be solved. They are meant to remind us that we live in a fallen world — and that even when we don't find, we must still seek."

That blend of grief and grace became part of the town's spiritual DNA. To this day, older parishioners in La Crosse still light candles on October 24 — not because they expect her return, but because they remember the feeling of a community holding its breath together.

The search for Evelyn had started as a rescue mission and ended as a kind of prayer.

The Weight of Never Knowing

Perhaps the hardest part for La Crosse wasn't what was found — it was what wasn't.

A body brings mourning. Evidence brings justice. But absence brings something far more difficult: imagination.

Every parent pictured what might have happened. Every teenager pictured how it must have felt. Every officer pictured where she might lie. In that way, Evelyn existed in thousands of versions, each one different, none complete.

Over the decades, that uncertainty became its own inheritance. For the children of La Crosse, Evelyn's story wasn't history — it was folklore with a date stamp. It whispered of the danger behind ordinary nights, of the line between the safe and the gone.

And so, even seventy years later, she remained not only part of the town's past, but its conscience.

A Presence That Outlasted Time

Today, the original Rasmusen house is gone. The neighborhood looks different — new trees, new windows, a generation that grew up without ever hearing the sound of 1950s sirens echoing across the Mississippi. But if you ask the right people, in the right tone, they'll still tell you about Evelyn Hartley.

They'll describe how she was smart, kind, musical. How she dreamed of becoming a teacher. How her father never stopped searching.

And then they'll lower their voices, as if she might still be nearby, listening.

Because in La Crosse, she is. Not as a ghost, not as a headline, but as a reminder. A reminder of what was lost, and of the quiet strength that comes from refusing to forget.

In the end, Evelyn Hartley's story is not about what was taken from her, but what she left behind — a legacy of vigilance, compassion, and the belief that even the smallest towns hold mysteries worth remembering.

CHAPTER 11 THE COLD CASE REVIVAL

By the turn of the twenty-first century, most of the people who had searched the bluffs and bridges for Evelyn Hartley were gone. Her parents had passed away, the detectives who once carried her photo in their wallets were buried, and the file that once sat on the police chief's desk now lived in an archive box labeled **"Cold Case 53-10 — HARTLEY, EVELYN GRACE."**

Yet somehow, the case still breathed.

In 2003, nearly fifty years after Evelyn vanished, a new generation of investigators—armed with technology their predecessors could only dream of—reopened the file. They called it a *review,* not a *reopening,* but for those who remembered, the distinction meant little. It was the first time in decades that someone had officially spoken her name inside the La Crosse Police Department with the word *investigation* attached to it.

A New Era of Tools

The revival began quietly when **Detective Mark Curtis**, then head of the department's cold case unit, stumbled across the Hartley files while cataloguing unsolved homicides. What struck him wasn't the lack of evidence—it was how *much* had been preserved.

Dozens of photos, dozens more handwritten notes. Original crime scene samples sealed in paper envelopes. Fragments of glass, fibers, and even dust scraped from the basement steps. The preservation was remarkably meticulous for 1953, the result of Chief Alforta's insistence that "we keep everything—because someday, science might make sense of what we can't."

That *someday* had arrived.

Curtis reached out to the Wisconsin State Crime Lab, asking whether the old blood samples—still sealed in glass vials— could yield usable DNA. The lab agreed to test them using modern amplification methods. To everyone's astonishment, *some material still contained viable cells.*

The First DNA Test

It was 2004 when the results came back. For the first time, Evelyn Hartley's genetic profile was entered into **CODIS**, the national DNA database. It was a ghostly kind of resurrection—her blood, drawn from the basement stains of the Rasmusen home, translated into digital code.

The hope was simple: that one day, a match might surface. A suspect's DNA entered for another crime might link back to those faint stains from 1953.

But no match came. The profile was partial, degraded by time. Enough to identify if remains were ever found—but not enough to identify a killer.

Still, the very act of typing it into the database felt monumental. "For the first time," Curtis said, "Evelyn's case wasn't just in a filing cabinet. It was in the system."

Revisiting the Evidence

The review went deeper than DNA. Using high-resolution scanners, investigators digitized all the original photographs. Modern software allowed them to enhance details that had once been invisible—the reflection of a lamp in the window glass, a faint shoe impression near the grass line. They consulted forensic imaging experts who determined the print was consistent with a man's heavy work boot, possibly size 10½ or 11—the same conclusion drawn decades earlier, but now confirmed with precision.

Technicians also examined the broken eyeglasses, using spectral analysis to determine trace elements in the blood. It confirmed the same blood type—O positive—but revealed minute particles of nickel, possibly from a metallic object. A belt buckle? A flashlight? The data suggested contact with something metallic at the moment of impact.

Even the basement dust was reexamined under microscopes, revealing fibers consistent with rough wool—perhaps from a coat.

Each new finding offered glimpses rather than answers. The case, like the river, remained murky.

The Media Rekindles the Flame

When the department quietly confirmed that the case had been re-evaluated using DNA, local media pounced. The *La Crosse Tribune* ran a Sunday feature titled:

"The Babysitter Case: Half a Century Later, Police Still Search for Answers."

It was 2005, and the article reignited a spark of collective memory. Former residents wrote letters. Retired officers called in with recollections. Someone mailed a yellowed photograph of a man at a gas station in 1953, claiming he had been seen "lingering near Coulee Drive."

National outlets took notice. *Dateline NBC* mentioned the case briefly in a segment on unsolved Midwestern disappearances. True crime forums—new digital gathering places for amateur sleuths—picked it up next. The internet gave Evelyn a second life.

Users on Websleuths and Reddit traded theories:

- Could the offender have been a traveling salesman?
- Was there a link to similar abductions across state lines?
- Did Peterson's "bridge confession" correspond to a specific GPS coordinate?

In the age of connectivity, Evelyn's case transformed from a regional mystery to a national cold case that anyone could investigate from their keyboard. For the first time, strangers across the country were talking about a fifteen-year-old girl from 1953 as if she were still missing yesterday.

The Forensic Future

By 2010, genealogical DNA analysis had revolutionized cold cases nationwide. Detectives re-examined whether the Hartley evidence could be used for **familial DNA searches**, comparing partial profiles to relatives of possible suspects. But degradation made the material unstable—too fragmented for the delicate sequencing required.

Still, the team retained hope. If ever Evelyn's remains were found, her profile could confirm her identity instantly. Her DNA, preserved in the database, would finally have the chance to speak for her.

Meanwhile, investigators explored another angle: digital composite aging. Using AI-based facial reconstruction, forensic artists created a "now" portrait of what Evelyn might look like if she had somehow survived and aged into her seventies. The rendering was placed in national missing persons databases—not because they believed she lived, but because hope has its own rituals.

A Voice from the Past

In 2013, on the sixtieth anniversary of her disappearance, a small ceremony was held at Riverside Park. About fifty people gathered —retired officers, teachers, and residents who remembered the original search. Detective Curtis stood at the microphone, holding a copy of the 1953 missing poster.

"She was never forgotten," he said. "Not by this town. Not by this department. And as long as this file exists, she never will be."

Then he read a letter written decades earlier by Evelyn's father, Richard Hartley:

"If she cannot come home, let her story stay alive long enough that someone learns from it. That will be her way of coming home."

The crowd fell silent. Some cried. For a moment, the river seemed to stop moving.

Still Waiting for the Match

As of today, Evelyn Hartley's case remains open—technically unsolved but perpetually active. Her DNA sits in national databases. Her photographs circulate among cold case investigators. Her name appears in training manuals as an example of both early investigative diligence and the evolution of forensic science.

Every few years, when advances in technology make headlines —touch DNA, environmental sampling, genealogical tracing— someone inevitably asks: *Could this finally solve the Hartley case?*

Maybe.

The bridge still stands. The river still moves. The questions still echo.

And in the crime lab archives of Madison, sealed in a small glass vial marked "Basement Stain Sample #2 — Hartley," rests a trace of blood that has outlived almost everyone who ever searched for her.

Science may yet find her voice.

Until then, the investigation remains what it has always been: a bridge between eras, between grief and justice, between silence and truth.

CHAPTER 12
THEORIES AND
SHADOWS

For every unsolved case, there are two stories: the one written in evidence, and the one written in speculation.

By the time Evelyn Hartley's disappearance reached its seventh decade, the official record had stopped growing—but the theories had not.

Each generation seemed to craft its own explanation, shaped as much by cultural fears as by facts. Some saw the work of a passing stranger, others a local man hiding in plain sight. Some envisioned a single predator; others whispered about two.

What unites them all is the same question that has haunted La Crosse since 1953: *Who took Evelyn, and how did he vanish with her so completely?*

The Local Opportunist

The first theory—and the one most investigators quietly favored—was the **local opportunist** hypothesis. It posited that Evelyn had been abducted by someone who knew the neighborhood, possibly even the Rasmusen family's routines.

Several factors supported this idea: the precision of the intrusion, the lack of noise, and the short time frame. The abductor had entered and exited the house without detection in a residential area where dogs barked at passing cars. He seemed to know when the Rasmusens would return and had enough confidence to act swiftly.

Police logs from 1953 noted several men living within a mile radius who had histories of burglary or assault. One in particular, a handyman with a history of voyeurism, was questioned repeatedly but never charged. His alibi was thin, but his connections in town—and lack of physical evidence—protected him.

Officers theorized that Evelyn might have resisted and been fatally injured inside the house, after which the perpetrator carried her body out through the basement door and into a vehicle parked nearby. The missing footprints in the dew, the dislodged window screen, and the trampled shrubbery all aligned with that possibility.

The tragedy of the "local man" theory was that, if true, the killer had likely lived the rest of his life within walking distance of the Rasmusen home—passing the site daily, unrecognized.

The Traveling Predator

The second major theory widened the lens. Some believed Evelyn was not the victim of a local man but of a **transient predator** passing through La Crosse.

In the early 1950s, U.S. Highway 14 ran close to the city, carrying truckers, salesmen, and drifters. The night Evelyn vanished, road patrol logs recorded several out-of-state vehicles stopping for fuel between La Crosse and Onalaska. The area also saw a rash of break-ins and attempted assaults in nearby towns during that same autumn, suggesting a pattern of mobility.

One name that appeared in later investigative notes was **Edward Wayne Edwards**—a notorious drifter and convicted murderer who had lived in Wisconsin in the 1950s. Decades later, some cold case researchers connected Edwards to numerous unsolved disappearances. While the timeline fit, no evidence ever placed him in La Crosse on October 24, 1953.

Still, the theory persists: a stranger who saw a light in a window, an opportunity, a brief struggle, and then gone.

The argument for this scenario lies in the clean disappearance—no witnesses, no car identified, no body. The argument against it lies in logistics: a stranger, unfamiliar with the neighborhood, would have risked far more. And yet, sometimes it is precisely the impulsive, irrational act that leaves the fewest traces.

The Two-Men Hypothesis

The third theory—what detectives privately called the **two-men hypothesis**—emerged from the earliest forensic inconsistencies.

Blood was found in multiple locations: inside the living room, near the basement, and outside by the window. For a single person to have inflicted the injuries, carried the body, and cleaned up, the timing would have been almost impossible within the estimated twenty-minute window between Evelyn's last phone check and the parents' arrival.

Investigators wondered if one man had entered the house while another waited outside. Several eyewitness reports from that night mentioned a dark car parked with its lights off near the corner of Coulee Drive. If true, the driver could have helped load the body or acted as lookout.

This theory also aligned with Clyde "Tywee" Peterson's taped confession in 1969, in which he mentioned "a buddy" helping him. But Peterson's unreliability—and the vagueness of his claim —made it impossible to verify.

Yet psychologically, the two-men theory explains much: the confidence, the speed, and the total disappearance. In criminology, pairs often commit crimes of opportunity that solo offenders would fear. The shared secret becomes its own twisted bond—strong enough to outlast fear, and sometimes even conscience.

The Stalker Connection

Another theory, favored by modern behavioral profilers, centers on **obsession** rather than opportunity.

Evelyn was not a random target, they argue. She was a fifteen-year-old honors student, intelligent, quiet, and deeply responsible —traits that may have attracted the attention of someone in her orbit. Perhaps a man who had seen her walking to Central High, who watched her daily and knew she babysat on Friday nights.

In this scenario, the abductor planned the event—not to kill, but to possess. The break-in, the cut screen, the missing shoe—all fit the pattern of a stalker who escalated from watching to taking.

Profiles drawn in the 2000s by the FBI's Behavioral Analysis Unit suggested that such offenders often lived alone, struggled with sexual deviance, and worked in jobs granting anonymity— janitors, delivery drivers, or repairmen.

If that profile is accurate, Evelyn's abductor may have continued living quietly, unseen, blending into Midwestern normalcy while carrying a secret too monstrous to name.

No such individual was ever conclusively identified. But among the men interviewed in 1953, several match that behavioral description disturbingly well.

The Bridge Theory

The final and most haunting theory is also the simplest: that Clyde Peterson told the truth, and Evelyn's body lies **near the bridge.**

"Buried by the bridge," he had said—the words that kept divers and detectives returning to the Mississippi for half a century.

Some investigators now believe that Peterson might have been closer to the truth than he realized—not because he was guilty, but because his drunken boast recycled something he had once *heard.* In small towns, secrets circulate like sediment; they settle, shift, and surface again.

Perhaps Peterson had overheard a real confession. Perhaps he had seen something he didn't fully understand.

Modern hydrological modeling supports the possibility that remains could have been buried in silt layers now twenty to thirty feet deep along Goose Island's floodplain. The currents of 1953 were far different than today's. A body placed near the waterline could have been swept downstream within hours, decomposing and dispersing long before morning light.

In this theory, Evelyn never left the bridge's shadow. She has been there all along—hidden not by cunning, but by the quiet persistence of the river.

The Psychology of the Unknown

Each theory reveals as much about human need as it does about evidence.

The local man theory satisfies the desire for accountability.

The drifter theory externalizes fear—evil comes from elsewhere.

The two-men theory offers logic to the impossible.

The stalker theory personalizes the horror.

The bridge theory romanticizes the mystery, letting nature itself hold the secret.

But behind every hypothesis lies one unchanging truth: no theory can fill the space Evelyn left behind.

Perhaps the man who took her died decades ago. Perhaps he confessed to no one. Perhaps, even now, there is someone in La Crosse who remembers a strange comment made long ago—a story that didn't sound like a story then, but does now.

In that way, Evelyn's case remains unsolved not because evidence failed, but because silence prevailed.

And silence, like the river, is patient.

CHAPTER 13 THE LEGACY OF FEAR AND FAITH

Every generation inherits its own kind of caution.

For the people of La Crosse, that inheritance began on an autumn night in 1953, when a girl named **Evelyn Hartley** walked into a stranger's house to babysit—and never walked out again.

Her story did not end with her disappearance. It expanded, rippled outward, reshaping the way parents raised children, the way police responded to danger, and the way America began to understand the fragility of safety itself.

In a sense, Evelyn's case was not just a tragedy—it was a turning point.

The End of Innocence

In the 1950s, America was wrapped in the illusion of safety. Suburbia was blooming; neighborhoods thrived on trust. Babysitting was an emblem of that innocence—a rite of passage for teenage girls.

Evelyn's disappearance shattered that illusion.

Before her, "missing children" were often assumed to be runaways or the victims of family disputes. After her, parents began to see that *ordinary life* could conceal extraordinary danger.

Sociologists later called the 1950s *the decade that lost its naivety.* It wasn't wars or politics that stripped it away—it was moments like this. A single unlocked door. A single light in a living room window. A single night that reminded the nation how fragile safety really was.

In La Crosse, that awareness became a kind of quiet religion. Families locked doors not out of paranoia, but out of reverence— for a girl whose story reminded them that evil doesn't always wear a stranger's face.

From Fear to Vigilance

By the 1960s and 1970s, Evelyn's case had become part of law enforcement training manuals in Wisconsin. Her disappearance illustrated the importance of immediate mobilization, neighborhood canvassing, and forensic preservation—all concepts ahead of their time in 1953.

The *Hartley Case Protocol*, as some officers informally called it, emphasized:

- Treat all missing minors as endangered from the outset.
- Secure the scene as both a potential crime scene and a rescue site.
- Document, preserve, and store all evidence, regardless of apparent relevance.

These principles would echo decades later in national legislation like the **Adam Walsh Child Protection Act (2006)** and the **Amber Alert system**, both built on the recognition that time and detail can mean the difference between disappearance and discovery.

Though Evelyn's name does not appear in those laws, her case stands as an early cautionary blueprint—a tragic forerunner of lessons written in hindsight.

The Influence on American Storytelling

When horror films and thrillers began populating screens in the 1970s and 1980s, critics noted a recurring theme: the babysitter alone, the phone call that never comes, the suburban home invaded.

It was fiction born from real fear—and in many ways, Evelyn's story was the original template.

When a Stranger Calls (1979), often cited as one of the earliest "babysitter horror" films, mirrored the exact tension of that October night: a girl tending someone else's child, a home that should have been safe, a disappearance that felt impossible.

Writers, consciously or not, were echoing a memory buried deep in America's cultural subconscious—a story passed through whispers, headlines, and community warnings. The fear of "the babysitter murder" had become symbolic, and Evelyn's ghost was woven into it.

But there's another side to this legacy: the way her story inspired *awareness*, not just fear. True crime writers, social scientists, and safety advocates began using her case as a teaching tool —to remind audiences that vigilance is not hysteria, and that remembering victims is a form of justice.

Faith as a Form of Memory

La Crosse is a city of churches, and in the years after Evelyn's disappearance, faith became both a refuge and a response. Congregations held vigils annually on October 24. Pastors spoke of light and darkness, of innocence and endurance.

For many, belief in God became the only way to live with the unanswered. "We had to find meaning," one woman said. "Otherwise, it would just be fear forever."

In sermons, Evelyn's story evolved from tragedy into parable. She represented the lost lamb, the one the shepherd searches for but cannot find. The message was not only about loss—it was about persistence, about seeking the missing with the same compassion with which faith seeks the unseen.

And perhaps that is why her name endured. Not because of the horror, but because of the humanity it evoked.

Even now, on the anniversary of her disappearance, candles still flicker in the windows of a few old houses on the south side of town. Some residents do it consciously; others inherited the ritual without remembering where it began.

The Lasting Symbol

Over seventy years later, Evelyn Hartley's story remains one of America's most haunting unsolved cases—not only because of its mystery, but because of its meaning.

She has become a symbol of vigilance, a reminder that darkness can hide in ordinary places—and that empathy is the light that answers it.

Her name is spoken in classrooms when teachers discuss personal safety. Her photo appears in documentaries about the evolution of criminal forensics. Her case is still cited in lectures on investigative persistence.

For the people of La Crosse, she is not just a victim; she is a thread connecting generations—between what was lost and what was learned.

In the words of a retired officer who spent his life chasing her shadow:

"We may never find her, but she found a way to change us."

That, in its own quiet way, is a kind of justice.

CHAPTER 14 THE RIVER KEEPS ITS SECRETS

At dusk, the Mississippi glows like a memory.

The bridges that cross it cast long shadows over the water, steel bones stretching from one shore to the next. If you stand on Pettibone Bridge long enough, you can hear the hum of tires overhead, the steady pulse of the city moving forward. But beneath that rhythm, if you listen closely, there is something else — the whisper of the current, restless and unending.

It is the same sound that filled the air the night Evelyn Hartley vanished.

The Weight of Water

Rivers hold history differently than land. They erase and preserve at once.

Every spring flood rearranges the earth, covering the old with the new, folding time upon itself. What is lost there doesn't disappear — it settles.

The searchers who combed the banks of Goose Island in the 1970s often said the same thing: "She's still here."

They didn't mean it as superstition. They meant it as faith — faith that the river remembers what people forget.

Over seventy years later, that faith has not faded.

Boaters still glance toward the shallows near the bridge. Fishermen still pause when they find a tangle of cloth in the mud. Divers who train in those waters still speak of an uneasy calm that descends the deeper they go. They don't call it fear. They call it respect.

The Passing of Time

La Crosse has changed. The old neighborhoods of Coulee Drive now blend into the modern sprawl of suburban life. The Rasmusen house, where Evelyn's shoes were found on the stairs, was torn down decades ago.

New families live there now, unaware that they walk each day over ground once marked by flashlights, search dogs, and silent prayer.

The detectives are gone. The files are digitized. The witnesses, those teenagers who once joined search parties in the woods, are grandparents or ghosts.

But every few years, a reporter still writes her name, and the letters come again — a man who thinks he saw something, a woman who recalls a rumor, a diver who found something strange. Most lead nowhere. Yet each one carries the same quiet confession: *We still want to know.*

The Bridge as a Metaphor

The title that locals gave her story — *The Bridge of Secrets* — was never about architecture. It was about connection. The bridge between past and present. Between the girl who vanished and the town that never stopped looking. Between fact and faith.

The Mississippi divides Wisconsin from Minnesota, but in the Hartley story it also divides certainty from silence.

One side is investigation — photographs, evidence, names. The other is everything unknowable — the moments after the porch light flickered, the footsteps that no one heard, the last breath swallowed by the night.

And somewhere between those two sides, suspended like the bridge itself, hangs the mystery.

A Voice in the Water

In 2019, a volunteer diver exploring near Goose Island found a piece of glass in the silt — old, clouded, square-cut. For a moment, he wondered if it might be part of Evelyn's eyeglasses. It wasn't. The lab dated it decades older, from a 1920s bottle. Still, the discovery made headlines.

People wanted to believe.

That is how Evelyn lives now — not as a file number, not as a photograph, but as a pulse that returns whenever the river rises.

Every time the water touches the banks where searchers once knelt, her name returns to the surface, if only for a moment.

What the River Knows

Perhaps the most haunting thing about Evelyn Hartley's story is not what remains unknown — but what remains *possible.*

Somewhere, beneath layers of silt and memory, there may still be an answer. A fragment of cloth. A trace of bone. A truth that waited for science or time or mercy.

And if the river could speak, maybe it would tell us:

"I saw it all. I carried her gently. I've kept her safe."

Maybe that's why the people of La Crosse stopped trying to conquer the river and started to coexist with it. The searches ended not because they lost faith, but because they accepted that some truths are larger than discovery.

The Mississippi is no longer just geography in this story. It is character, witness, and tomb. It is the keeper of the last secret.

The Girl Who Still Walks Home

In the end, Evelyn remains forever fifteen — frozen in that October dusk, stepping through the Rasmusen doorway with her books and quiet smile. The porch light still burns in imagination, her shadow crossing the threshold like a promise that she'll return.

And maybe, in the way memory works, she has.

Every act of vigilance, every search for a missing person, every parent who teaches a child to stay alert — all of them carry a fragment of her legacy.

The story of Evelyn Hartley isn't about how she died. It's about how a community learned to care harder, look longer, and love with the ache of never knowing.

Time moved on, but her light never went out.

EPILOGUE

— *The Bridge Still Stands*

If you stand on the bridge at sunset, the river below turns gold.

The Mississippi does this without ceremony, as it always has—catching the last light of day and breaking it into fragments that drift and disappear. The air smells faintly of pine and rust, of water and age, of stories carried longer than memory. Traffic hums overhead, steady and indifferent. Life continues, as it must.

But when the wind shifts, there is another sound beneath it all.

Flashlights cutting through the dark.

Boots on wet ground.

Voices calling a name that never answered back.

They never found her.

For decades, that sentence has sat heavy in La Crosse—spoken carefully, as though saying it too loudly might summon something unbearable. Evelyn Hartley vanished into the space between what could be known and what never was. No grave. No final moment witnessed. No place to kneel with certainty.

And yet—perhaps that was never the end of the story.

Perhaps the finding was never the point.

Because Evelyn did not disappear from this town. She changed it.

In La Crosse, every October, the river still glimmers as if holding something just beneath the surface—something precious, something unfinished, something waiting. Parents double-check doors. Teenagers are driven home from babysitting jobs. Officers treat every missing child as urgent, not assumed. Searchers remember to look one more time.

Her absence became a presence.

The bridges still span the water, connecting one shore to the next, holding weight without complaint. They do what bridges are meant to do: endure, even when they carry grief. Beneath them, the river keeps moving—quiet, patient, unrevealing.

It keeps its secrets.

And so, too, does she.

Evelyn Hartley remains fifteen years old in memory—walking into a house lit warmly against the October dark, doing an ordinary kindness that should never have cost her life. She remains a name spoken softly, a photograph held carefully, a question that refuses to fade.

Not all mysteries are solved.

Not all stories are closed.

Some remain—not to torment, but to remind.

That vigilance matters.

That memory matters.

That even when answers are withheld, responsibility is not.

The river flows on.

The bridge still stands.

And Evelyn—though never found—was never lost to time.

She is here, in the remembering.

A PERSONAL REQUEST

Thank you for reading *The Bridge of Secrets: The Murder of Evelyn Hartley*.

If this book stayed with you—if it made you pause, reflect, or see this case in a new way—I would be deeply grateful if you left a review. A written review is always appreciated, but even selecting a star rating—without writing anything further— helps more than you might realize. It signals to bookstores and reading platforms that this story matters and that careful, victim-centered true crime has a place.

If you'd like to leave a review, you can visit the Amazon page here: *The Bridge of Secrets: The Murder of Evelyn Hartley*

Or simply scan the QR code below to go directly to the review page.

Your support helps ensure that Evelyn Hartley's story—and the unanswered questions that still surround it—are not forgotten.

With gratitude,

Linda Davidson

ALSO BY THE AUTHOR

AUTHOR'S NOTE

Evelyn Grace Hartley (1938–missing since October 24, 1953) was a real fifteen-year-old girl from La Crosse, Wisconsin. This book honors her life and the decades of effort by family, neighbors, officers, divers, searchers, reporters, and volunteers who refused to forget her.

This narrative blends **documented history** (contemporary reporting, official statements, archived photographs, interviews, and public records) with **careful literary reconstruction**: the sounds of a stadium, the angle of a lamp, the feel of a cold riverbank at night. Wherever the text moves beyond the archival record—describing sensory detail or private thought—it does so to carry readers more fully into the documented time and place. No invented fact is presented as fact; reconstruction serves clarity and empathy, never sensationalism.

A final note of gratitude: to the people of La Crosse who kept Evelyn's story alive in memory, in practice, and in community. May her name continue to be spoken with tenderness—and may diligence on behalf of missing children everywhere be part of her legacy.

— **Linda Davidson**

ACKNOWLEDGMENTS

This book exists because a young girl's name refused to disappear.

To the Hartley family—who carried Evelyn's absence through decades that offered no answers, only anniversaries—thank you for the quiet, enduring example of love that does not expire. The ache of not knowing is its own kind of lifelong labor. Your persistence, your dignity, and your refusal to let Evelyn become "just a case" shaped the heart of this work.

To the Rasmusen family—whose home became the unwanted center of a tragedy no one could have imagined—thank you for the human grace it takes to live inside a story the public repeats. When crime enters a house, it doesn't only take a victim; it takes a sense of safety, and it leaves behind questions that settle into walls. Your lives were changed, too, and your place in this history is acknowledged with respect.

To La Crosse law enforcement across generations—patrol officers, deputies, detectives, supervisors, dispatchers, and those who inherited the file long after the first search lights went dark —thank you for the work that rarely gets romanticized: the paperwork, the interviews, the revisited leads, the evidence preservation, the difficult decisions made under pressure, and the humility of continuing even when the trail went cold. Some of you carried Evelyn's photo in your memory the way others carry a prayer. This book honors that determination, even when the outcome was not the one you fought for.

To the searchers—National Guard members, Civil Air Patrol crews, Boy Scouts, firefighters, pilots, divers, volunteers, and ordinary citizens who walked the bluffs and riverbanks—thank you for showing what a community looks like when it refuses to stand still in the face of fear. You gave your weekends, your strength, your breath in the cold air, and your hope. Many of you returned again and again, not because you were certain you'd find something, but because a child was missing and that fact demanded action. That matters.

To local librarians, archivists, and custodians of memory—especially those who preserved fragile clippings, photographs, and records long after public attention moved elsewhere—thank you for holding history carefully. In cold cases, the archive becomes a second crime scene, and your patience becomes a form of justice. Because you kept what others might have discarded, later generations still have something to study, question, and learn from.

To responsible journalists, editors, and researchers who approached this case with restraint—who remembered that a headline is not the same as a life—thank you for documenting without turning suffering into spectacle. When reporting is done with care, it protects the dignity of the missing and the living alike.

To cold case investigators everywhere: your work is a kind of vigil. You enter rooms of silence and try to make them speak. You read old pages until you can hear the people behind them. You stand in the gap between what happened and what can be proven. Even when the world calls a case "old," you treat it as present—because for a family, it always is. This book is written in solidarity with that mission.

And to readers—your attention is a choice. In a world that moves fast and forgets easily, you chose to stay with a story that is unresolved, uncomfortable, and human. Thank you for reading with compassion, for holding space for uncertainty, and for remembering Evelyn as more than a name tied to a mystery. If this book leaves you with anything, I hope it is this: remembrance is not passive. It is an act of care.

With gratitude,

Linda Davidson

NOTE ON SOURCES
& METHOD

Primary sources included contemporary newspaper coverage; municipal records; law-enforcement memos and public statements; aerial and site photographs; oral histories and interviews given in later decades by searchers and officers; and regional histories of La Crosse and the Upper Mississippi River.

Secondary sources included scholarly work on mid-century forensic practice (serology, latent print techniques), cold-case methodology, hydrology of the Mississippi backwaters, offender behavior, and case studies of parallel disappearances.

Where multiple versions of an event existed, I favored **earliest contemporaneous accounts** and **corroborated points** across independent sources. Rumors and legends appear in this book only when they materially shaped the investigation or community memory; they are clearly labeled as such.

CONTENT INTEGRITY STATEMENT

- **No composite suspects**: Individuals are referenced as they appeared in public record, investigative notes, or reported testimony.
- **No invented evidence**: All physical and procedural details attributed to the investigation have an archival basis.
- **Reconstruction boundary**: Ambience, dialogue cadence, and interior states are rendered as literary reconstruction and never intended to override the record.
- **Respect for living persons**: The book avoids naming non-charged, living private individuals except where already a matter of sustained public record and strictly necessary to the history.

CHRONOLOGY KEY DATES

- **October 24, 1953 (Fri.)** — Evelyn babysits at the Rasmusen home; last confirmed movement ~7:15 p.m.; unanswered calls begin ~8:30 p.m.; house discovered disturbed ~10:45–11:00 p.m.
- **Oct 25–Nov 1953** — Massive search: roadblocks, air patrol, river/field sweeps; early blood evidence typed (O).
- **Winter 1953–1954** — Polygraph program on local males/students; no actionable result.
- **1957** — Ed Gein investigated and publicly cleared in relation to the Hartley case.
- **1969–1970s** — "Bar-tape confession" surfaces; renewed digs and dives near bridges/backwaters.
- **1980s** — Intermittent riverbank finds (non-evidentiary), private searches, and media revivals.
- **2003–2010s** — Cold case review; digitization; limited DNA profiling from preserved samples; entry to national databases; commemorations continue.
- **Present** — Case open; evidence archived; periodic reviews as technology advances.

EVIDENCE SUMMARY (READER'S REFERENCE)

Scene Indicators

- Removed basement window screen; small interior disarray; broken prescription eyeglasses with displaced lens.
- Bloodstaining (typed O) on basement steps/interior surfaces and exterior grass line.
- Partial footwear impression consistent with a men's work boot (~10–11).

Search Operations

- Ground grids; air sorties; river drags; vehicle checkpoints; canvasses; school-based interviews and polygraphs.

Lead Categories

- Local persons of interest; traveling/transient actors; two-offender hypotheses; bridge/backwater burial theory.

Limitations

- Pre-DNA serology; limited latent print usefulness; weather/trampling degradation; absence of recovered remains.

SUSPECT & LEAD DOSSIERS (CONCISE)

- **Ed Gein (1957)** — Questioned due to proximity and notoriety; cleared; no physical linkage; alibi/witness corroboration.
- **Clyde "Tywee" Peterson (1969 tape)** — Alcohol-mediated statements implying involvement and "bridge" burial; inconsistent interviews; insufficient corroboration; deceased 1974.
- **Unnamed Local Handyman(s)** — Questioned in 1953–54; alibis tenuous; no evidentiary bridge to charge.
- **Transient/Traveling Offender Theory** — Fits mobility and vanishing; less consistent with precise, quiet entry.

FORENSICS THEN & NOW (PLAIN-LANGUAGE GUIDE)

1953 Capabilities

- ABO blood typing; powder dusting for prints; shoe-print photography; canvassing; polygraph in wide, controversial use.

Modern Options (If Materials Survive)

- Touch DNA & M-VAC collection; mitochondrial/nuclear DNA from micro-traces; genealogy-assisted investigative leads; advanced footwear/trace pattern analysis; soil/environmental eDNA; enhanced audio for legacy recordings; hydrological modeling for silt burial zones; GPR & cadaver dogs for floodplain anomalies.

READER FAQ

Is there a definitive suspect?

No. Multiple leads were explored; none reached the threshold for charge or closure.

Could DNA solve this?

Possibly—if suitable biological material is found or preserved remains are recovered.

Why "bridge" and "river" recur as motifs?

Because they are both physical search loci and living metaphors for connection and secrecy in this case.

LANGUAGE, NAMES, AND ETHICS

- Names of private individuals are minimized unless long established in public record.
- Period language is maintained in quotes for historical accuracy; harmful terms are not endorsed and are contextualized by era.

ORGANIZATIONS & RESOURCES

- **National Center for Missing & Exploited Children** — education, prevention, and support.
- **NamUs (National Missing and Unidentified Persons System)** — public database for missing/unidentified cases.
- **State Crime Laboratory / Cold Case Units** — for updates on legacy case practices and submissions.

(When engaging with agencies or databases, please follow their current submission and contact guidelines.)

DISCUSSION & BOOK-CLUB GUIDE

1. How does uncertainty shape a community differently than a solved tragedy?
2. Where do caution and fear diverge—and how can communities choose caution without surrendering to fear?
3. Which theory did you find most plausible, and what evidence (or absence of evidence) swayed you?
4. How do bridges and rivers operate as both physical settings and metaphors throughout the book?
5. What responsibilities do writers and readers bear when engaging with true crime?

REMEMBERING EVELYN

If this book moved you, let it move you toward **care**: check on neighbors, support local search-and-rescue and victim services, teach children practical safety without panic, and honor the missing by learning their names. For Evelyn, remembrance is an act of love and a promise that vigilance endures.

ABOUT THE AUTHOR

Linda Davidson is a true crime author who writes for readers who want more than shock value — they want truth with a heartbeat.

She focuses on the kinds of stories that stay with you long after the news cameras leave: unsolved murders, missing persons, rural disappearances, and investigations that never received clear answers. Instead of chasing sensational headlines, Linda writes with one question in mind: *How can I honor the victim and still tell the full truth of what happened?*

In each book, she blends careful research, clear timelines, and compassionate storytelling. Readers are guided through evidence, leads, theories, and dead ends in a way that is easy to follow and emotionally grounded. Her work keeps the victim at the center of the narrative while also examining the failures, gaps, and human decisions that shaped each case.

Linda's books are written for true crime readers who care about people, not just plot twists. She writes for those who feel frustrated by shallow coverage and are hungry for deeper, more thoughtful explorations of the cases that haunt them.

Her promise is simple:

She will research carefully.

She will explain clearly.

She will tell the truth with respect.

She will never forget that the people she writes about were real.

Linda Davidson is a true crime author dedicated to telling

the stories others forget. She writes about unsolved murders, mysterious disappearances, and cold cases with a focus on the victims, their families, and the communities left behind. Combining deep research with compassionate storytelling, she helps readers make sense of complex investigations without losing sight of the human beings at the center of every case.

PERMISSIONS

All photographs, quotations, and reproduced materials are used with permission where required or rely on fair use for purposes of commentary, scholarship, and historical documentation. Every effort has been made to trace rights holders; any omissions are unintentional, and corrections will be incorporated in subsequent editions.

INDEX (ABRIDGED)

END NOTE

— Light in the Dark

Stories like this one walk us through some of the darkest places a human heart can go. It is easy to believe that evil has the last word—that violence, corruption, or indifference are stronger than anything else.

The Bible says something different. It tells us that God sees every unseen hurt, hears every unheard prayer, and judges every hidden deed. It also says that no life is beyond His reach, and no story is too broken to be redeemed. Justice matters to God. So does mercy. So does you.

If what you've read has stirred fear, anger, or regret in your own heart, know this: the door back to Him is never closed. Repentance is simply turning around and letting Him meet you where you are.

"Do not be overcome by evil, but overcome evil with good."

— Romans 12:21

"The light shines in the darkness, and the darkness has not overcome it."

— John 1:5

May these pages not only expose what went wrong, but also awaken a hunger for what is right—for justice, for truth, and for the kind of grace that can still save a soul.

REFERENCES

1. A&E Television Networks. (2025, September 17). *The mysterious disappearance of Evelyn Hartley—and whether serial killer Ed Gein played a role.* A&E.

2. Associated Press. (1953, October–November). *Coverage of the disappearance of Evelyn Hartley* [News reports]. Associated Press Archives.

3. Casefile Presents. (2021). *Case 224: Evelyn Hartley* [Audio podcast episode]. In *Casefile True Crime.* Casefile Presents.

4. Hessel, S. T. (2005). *Where's Evelyn? The 1953 babysitter's kidnapping that shook the nation.* Lessons from Life Publications.

5. La Crosse Public Library Archives. (n.d.). *Evelyn Hartley* (History Repeats: Local History feature). La Crosse Public Library.

6. National Missing and Unidentified Persons System. (n.d.). *Missing person case: Hartley, Evelyn Grace (NamUs #MP4579).* U.S. Department of Justice.

7. Open Road Media. (2018, July 25). *The babysitter who vanished: What happened to Evelyn Hartley?* The Lineup.

8. Turney, S. (2025, October 9). *Evelyn Hartley* [Case article and episode notes]. *Voices for Justice.* Voices for Justice LLC.

9. The Vanished Podcast. (2017). *Evelyn Hartley* [Audio podcast episode]. In *The Vanished Podcast.*

10. Wikipedia contributors. (n.d.). *Disappearance of Evelyn Hartley.* In *Wikipedia.* Wikimedia Foundation. Retrieved

January 14, 2026, from https://en.wikipedia.org/wiki/
Disappearance_of_Evelyn_Hartley

SUGGESTED FURTHER READING

Contemporary & Archival Newspaper Reporting

La Crosse Tribune. (1953, October–December). *[Coverage of the disappearance and investigation of Evelyn Grace Hartley].*

La Crosse Tribune. (1960s–2010s). *[Anniversary and retrospective reporting on the Evelyn Hartley case].*

Chicago Tribune. (1953–1954). *[Regional coverage of the Evelyn Hartley disappearance and search efforts].*

Chicago Tribune. (Later decades). *[Retrospective mentions and summaries of the Evelyn Hartley case].*

Wisconsin State Journal. (1953–1954). *[Statewide reporting on the Evelyn Hartley investigation].*

Wisconsin State Journal. (Later decades). *[Retrospective coverage of the Evelyn Hartley cold case].*

Local History & Archival Sources

La Crosse Public Library Archives. (n.d.). *Local history files on the disappearance of Evelyn Grace Hartley.* La Crosse, WI.

La Crosse Public Library Archives. (n.d.). *Photograph collections and newspaper clipping files related to mid-century La Crosse.* La Crosse, WI.

La Crosse County Historical Society. (n.d.). *Regional history materials and community records.* La Crosse, WI.

La Crosse Police Department. (n.d.). *Historical summaries and public press materials related to the Hartley investigation.*

La Crosse County Sheriff's Office. (n.d.). *Public-domain historical records and investigative summaries.*
Forensics & Cold Case Investigation

Inman, K., Rudin, N., & Cheng, K. (2002). *Principles and practice of criminalistics: The profession of forensic science.* CRC Press.

Saferstein, R. (2018). *Criminalistics: An introduction to forensic science* (12th ed.). Pearson.

Wecht, C. H. (2006). *Forensic science and law: Investigative applications in criminal justice.* Quorum Books.

Federal Bureau of Investigation. (n.d.). *Cold case investigation standards and evidence preservation practices.* FBI.

Butler, J. M. (2015). *Advanced topics in forensic DNA typing: Interpretation.* Academic Press.
Criminology & Victimology

Douglas, J. E., Burgess, A. W., Burgess, A. G., & Ressler, R. K. (1992). *Crime classification manual.* Lexington Books.

Turvey, B. E. (2012). *Criminal profiling: An introduction to behavioral evidence analysis* (4th ed.). Academic Press.

Karmen, A. (2016). *Crime victims: An introduction to victimology* (9th ed.). Cengage Learning.
Cultural Memory & Media Studies

Jackson, M. (2009). *Distracted souls: Psychiatric histories and the crisis of attention.* Oxford University Press.

Furedi, F. (2006). *Culture of fear revisited: Risk-taking and the morality of low expectation.* Continuum.

Schmid, D. (2005). *Natural born celebrities: Serial killers in American culture.* University of Chicago Press.